MERINGUE

MERINGUE

LINDA K. JACKSON & JENNIFER EVANS GARDNER

Photographs by Alexandra DeFurio

GIBBS SMITH
TO ENRICH AND INSPIRE HUMANKIND

First Edition
16 15 14 13 12   5 4 3 2 1

Published by
Gibbs Smith
P.O. Box 667
Layton, Utah 84041

1.800.835.4993 orders
www.gibbs-smith.com

Designed by Rita Sowins/Sowins Design
Food styling by Anni Daulter, Delicious Gratitude
Printed and bound in Hong Kong
Gibbs Smith books are printed on paper produced from sustainable PEFC-
certified forest/controlled wood source. Learn more at www.pefc.org.

Library of Congress Cataloging-in-Publication Data

Jackson, Linda K.
Meringue / Linda K. Jackson and Jennifer Evans Gardner;
photographs by Alexandra DeFurio. — 1st ed.
p. cm.
ISBN 978-1-4236-2581-0
1. Cooking (Meringue) I. Gardner, Jennifer Evans. II. Title.
TX745.J35 2012
641.81'5—dc23
2012004321

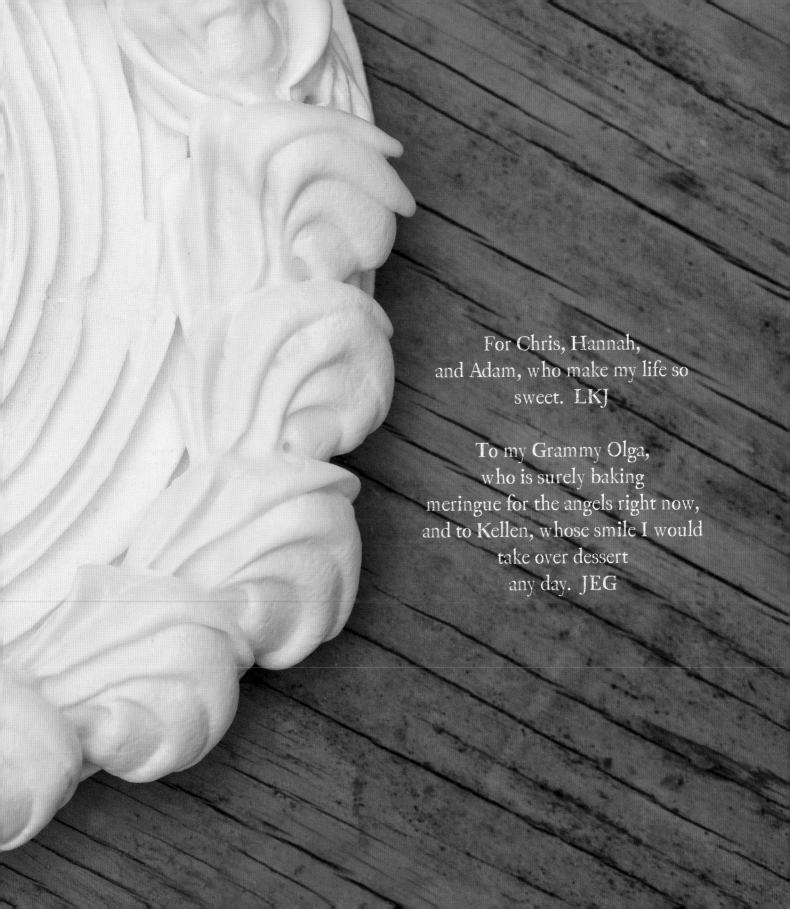

For Chris, Hannah,
and Adam, who make my life so
sweet. LKJ

To my Grammy Olga,
who is surely baking
meringue for the angels right now,
and to Kellen, whose smile I would
take over dessert
any day. JEG

CONTENTS

ACKNOWLEDGMENTS

We would like to thank our families and friends for their love and encouragement, and for so selflessly offering to taste our creations during recipe development. Most of all, thanks to Paul, Arianne, Cleo, Henry, Oliver, Dawn, Pete, Laura, Ezekiel, Papo, Mike, Alex, Cyndi, Mark, Pha, June, Jessica, Victoria, and Owen.

Special thanks to our fantastic editor (and fellow brown sugar thief) Michelle Branson and the entire Gibbs Smith team; the brilliant Alexandra DeFurio and Anni Daulter for creating the most gorgeous meringue photos ever; Karen Kaplan for her generous suggestions and Steven Krakowsky for his wise counsel; our agent Deborah Ritchken for being the first to fall in love with our meringue cookbook and for finding it a home; the Neighborhood School for bringing us together lo so many years ago, and finally, our mothers Dolores and Dorothy, who still make the best lemon meringue pies we've ever tasted.

ST CARD

FOR ADDRESS ONLY

PONDENCE

Moonlight & Roses

INTRODUCTION

Egg whites. Sugar. A pinch of cream of tartar or a dash of vinegar. And air.

Meringue. How can something be so simple, so divine, and yet so intimidating at the same time?

We both fell in love with meringue the same way. Though we grew up thousands of miles apart, it was the first bite of our mothers' lemon meringue pies, the fluffy topping still warm from the oven atop sweet lemon curd that made us swoon. But it was years before we fully realized how many different forms meringue could take—and we were hooked for life. For Linda, it was the addictive meringue gelato at the world famous gelateria Vivoli in Florence; for Jennifer, it was a cloud-light meringue torte, le Vacherin, while living in Paris.

Our paths finally merged at a potluck "feast" at our children's preschool. We spotted the desserts first—Linda's tiny, light-as-a-cloud meringue cookies flecked with chocolate and Jennifer's raspberry meringue tartlets—amidst the store-bought cakes, cookies, and one sad frozen lasagna. As the adults elbowed their toddlers out of the way to get to our desserts, our eyes met, smiles in check. It was friendship at first sight.

We always get the same reaction when we serve meringues. It seems that because they are so delicate and look so elegant, everyone—even our friends who are experienced bakers—assumes they are difficult to make. Not so. They may look intimidating, but they are actually quite simple to make. Even those with little or no baking experience can quickly master meringue.

Meringue is magical. It is incredibly versatile. It can be spooned onto pies, or piped into any number of beautiful shapes. It can be baked or poached, whipped into silky frostings, or folded into cakes to make them fluffier. It can be combined with ground nuts, chocolate, or any number of flavorings. It can be formed into various vessels for chantilly cream and fresh berries. And that's just the beginning. We hope this book will encourage you to embrace meringue as we have, and that it inspires you to make heavenly creations of your very own.

About Meringue

A Bit of History

Meringue isn't just magical. It's mysterious. No one can quite agree on its origins (and here's a hint: it wasn't invented in France). According to the *Larousse Gastronomique: The New American Edition of the World's Greatest Culinary Encyclopedia*:

Some historians of cookery believe that the meringue was invented by a Swiss pastry cook called Gasparini, who practiced his art in the small town of Meiringen (now in East Germany). Others maintain that the word comes from the Polish word marzynka and that the preparation was invented by a chef in the service of King Stanislas I Leszcynski, who later became Duke of Lorraine. The king passed on the recipe to his daughter, Marie, who introduced it to the French. Queen Marie Antoinette had a great liking for meringues and court lore has it that she made them with her own hands at the Trianon, where she is also said to have made vacherins, which are prepared from a similar mixture.

While most food historians confirm Marie Antoinette's love of meringues, some say that meringue goes back to a much earlier date . . . and that it was invented in England, of all places. The earliest documented recipe for a baked "beaten-egg-white-and-sugar confection" is the handwritten recipe for White Bisket Bread by Lady Elinor Fettiplace in 1604 in Oxfordshire, which later appeared in the cookbook *Elinor Fettiplace's Receipt Book —Elizabethan Country House Cooking*.

Historians do agree on this: Until the early nineteenth century, meringues cooked in the oven were shaped with a spoon. It was the great French pastry chef Antoine Carême who first used a piping (pastry) bag.

We know one thing for certain: meringue is deceptively simple, and once you know the basics, you can create sweet magic with meringue cookies, Pavlovas, pies, tarts—even marjolaines and dacquoises.

And Some Science . . .

But first, a note about that magic—or the science—of meringue. Exactly how do egg whites turn into voluminous cloud-like confections, anyway? In simple laymen's terms (as we aren't scientists), beating an egg white causes the proteins to unfold, after which it recombines into a new structure around air bubbles, creating volume.

Adding acid, such as cream of tartar or vinegar, slows coagulation so that more air can be added, and the whipped egg whites can expand to as much as eight times their original volume.

Adding sugar helps stabilize the beaten egg whites and helps them hold their shape. In the meantime, sugar pulls the water from the egg whites, allowing them to set up better.

When meringues are cooked or baked, the steam created by the heat causes the air bubbles to expand even more, creating greater volume.

FOAMY

SOFT PEAKS

STIFF PEAKS

The Three Stages of Meringue

Whether whisking by hand or with an electric mixer, egg whites go through various stages to become meringue: Foamy, soft peaks, and stiff peaks. Some cookbooks also reference "medium peaks," however, as the stage just before stiff peaks is so subtle in its difference, we found that it wasn't relevant.

FOAMY
The egg whites will still be a liquid, they may have a cloudy yellow color, and large bubbles will have formed.

SOFT PEAKS
The egg whites will become snowy white, and as your whisk moves through the meringue, you'll see ribbons or lines from the wires of the whisk. At this point, with the mixer running, you will slowly begin to add sugar, about 1 tablespoon at a time. When you pull your whisk up from the bowl, a peak will form but won't hold its shape for long.

STIFF PEAKS
All of the sugar will have been incorporated, and you will continue to beat the meringue until it reaches its full volume. It will now be thick, smooth, and glossy. When you lift the whisk from the bowl, the peaks will completely hold their shape.

The Three Types of Meringue

Meringue can be eaten in soft or hard form, and can be prepared using three different methods: French, Italian, and Swiss.

FRENCH MERINGUE

Fine white sugar is beaten into room temperature egg whites until peaks are stiff and glossy. It is the simplest of the three methods and is used in the majority of the recipes in this book.

ITALIAN MERINGUE

This type of meringue is made by boiling a sugar syrup and then whipping it into stiffly beaten egg whites until stiff and glossy. This creates a very stable soft meringue. For those concerned about eating raw eggs, this type of meringue is safe to use without further baking.

SWISS MERINGUE

Egg whites and sugar are whisked over a double boiler or *bain marie* to warm them, and then the mixture is whipped with an electric mixer into stiff, glossy peaks. Similar to Italian meringue, the egg whites in this method are also cooked and safe to eat without further baking.

The Virtues of Meringue

Meringue isn't just another pretty face in the world of sweets. Because they are made with only the whites of eggs, they are low in fat and high in protein. Basic meringue contains no flour or dairy, making it the perfect dessert for those on special gluten-free or lactose-free diets. There are no leavening agents in meringue, so the majority of desserts in this book can be made for Passover as well.

What Are You Waiting For?

Meringue may be the perfect dessert, but it doesn't have to look "perfect," so if that is holding you back, let it go. It will taste great, no matter what. If it cracks, who cares? Crumble it up and toss it with freshly whipped cream and fruit to create an Eton Mess. Our philosophy is that there are no "mess ups" when it comes to meringue. You're eating a cloud, after all. That's perfection enough.

Ingredients, Tools, and Techniques

Basic Ingredients

EGG WHITES

All meringue recipes start with egg whites. You'll find that egg whites foam best when they're at room temperature. (More on that in the Tips and Techniques section.) You might be surprised to learn that frozen egg whites, thawed to room temperature, also whip up beautifully. If you make a recipe that calls for more egg yolks than whole eggs (like a custard or curd), you can freeze the whites to use later for meringues. While it might be very tempting to use store-bought pasteurized liquid egg whites, it's not a good idea because the heat of the pasteurization process can prevent the egg whites from foaming fully and developing a stable meringue. Some liquid egg white packages specifically note that they should not be used for meringues.

SUGAR

We recommend using superfine sugar because each granule is small and it incorporates and dissolves easily into the egg whites. You can find superfine sugar, also known as bakers' sugar (or caster sugar as the Brits call it), in the baking section of your grocery store. You can also make it yourself by pulsing regular granulated sugar in a food processor fitted with the metal blade for about 2 minutes. Be sure to cover the opening at the top of the food processor with your hand or a dishtowel since the small sugar particles tend to float away. If all this sounds like too much trouble, simply use regular sugar. Just make sure to beat your meringue long enough that the sugar dissolves (but not too long or your meringue will dry out). Some of our recipes call for brown sugar or powdered sugar (also known as confectioners' sugar), alone or in addition to superfine sugar. Brown sugar gives the meringues a wonderful caramel flavor while powdered sugar yields a particularly light meringue. And here's a cautionary tale for all of you hoping to save calories by using a sugar substitute instead of sugar: DON'T DO IT! Your meringue will come out like rubber! We learned that lesson the hard way.

CREAM OF TARTAR

If you were a chemistry major in college, you'll know it as Potassium Hydrogen Tartrate. The rest of us know it by another odd, but easier to pronounce name, cream of tartar. A by-product of wine making, it's an acid that has an important role in meringue recipes: to help stabilize and give more volume to the beaten egg whites. Note, because brown sugar is naturally acidic, our recipes in which brown sugar is used do not include cream of tartar.

VINEGAR

Vinegar is an acid sometimes used in meringues instead of cream of tartar. (Don't worry; your dessert won't taste like salad dressing.) We typically use white wine or distilled white vinegar in our recipes.

SALT

Some recipes call for salt, which is primarily for flavor. Because it can decrease the stability of the beaten egg whites, it shouldn't be added too early.

CORNSTARCH

A little bit of cornstarch can play an important role of keeping the meringue from shrinking when baked. This is particularly important when making soft meringues as pie toppings since the tendency is for the meringue to shrink and pull away from the crust. It can also add to the stability of meringues. You may want to try the technique of whisking the cornstarch into the sugar to be added during the soft peak stage, rather than adding it at the end.

Tools

EGG SEPARATOR

Linda swears by a handy little plastic egg-separating tool she received as a parting gift at a Tupperware party 25 years ago. Tupperware has since discontinued this item, but similar ones are available online and in select specialty stores. But if you don't have one, don't worry since you can easily separate eggs without a special tool, as described in the Tips and Techniques section.

METAL BOWLS

Because plastic bowls can harbor traces of oil and fat and aluminum bowls can turn egg whites gray, they are not recommended for beating meringue. Copper bowls are often recommended because the whites react with the copper, creating greater volume for your meringue; however, for most people, copper isn't practical because of the expense and care involved. Our favorite vessel for beating meringue is a stainless steel bowl. In fact, the stainless steel bowls of our standing electric mixers are what we always use with great success.

STANDING ELECTRIC MIXER WITH WHISK ATTACHMENT

There's nothing quite like a standing electric mixer for all your baking needs. These power-houses (also referred to as an electric stand mixer or simply a stand mixer), when fitted with the whisk attachment, dramatically cut the amount of time it takes to beat egg whites and create meringues with great volume. If you don't own a stand mixer, you can also use a hand-held electric mixer, though it will take slightly longer to whip up your meringue. Actually, a hand-held mixer is an essential tool when making some frosting recipes that call for beating whites and sugar on the stovetop.

PARCHMENT PAPER AND SILICONE MATS

Meringues are delicate, so it's important that they are baked on a surface that will make them easy to remove. Never put unbaked meringue directly on a baking sheet; instead line the sheet with parchment paper (available at grocery stores). Since the parchment will tend to curl up, you can secure it to the metal baking sheet with a dab of the meringue on the bottom of each corner of the parchment, or you can use some masking tape. A silicone mat (such as Silpat) will work, if you prefer, and, in a pinch, you can also line your baking sheet with aluminum foil.

Note: Because meringues don't spread when they bake, you can fit more cookies on a baking sheet than you typically would.

CANDY THERMOMETER

You'll need one of these when making Italian and French meringues.

PASTRY BAGS, COUPLERS, AND TIPS

Some recipes call for you to pipe the meringue. If you have cloth or disposable plastic pastry bags, great. If not, try using a plastic ziplock bag with one of the corners cut off. Couplers and pastry bag tips are great tools when you are piping decorative shapes. Couplers are inserted inside the pastry bag and then the tip is attached to the outside, making it a breeze to change tips whenever you want a different shape or texture. Both couplers and tips are available in different sizes. Piping with star tips not only make beautiful meringue cookies, they also can create gorgeous Pavlovas and pretty patterns on desserts such as Baked Alaska.

MESH TEA BALL OR FINE MESH COLANDER

It's always fun to find new uses for kitchen items. Small mesh balls, originally intended for brewing tea leaves, are ideal for dusting a bit of powdered sugar or cocoa powder over desserts. Simply fill the ball with a bit of sugar or cocoa then give it a light, back and forth shake for a fine dusting of powder without any lumps. You can also use a fine mesh colander—just put a bit of sugar or cocoa into the colander and gently shake it over your dessert.

Tips and Techniques

MOISTURE IS THE ENEMY

Not only will humidity give you a bad hair day, it can lead to a soggy, sticky meringue. That's because sugar—one of the main ingredients in every meringue recipe—attracts moisture from the air. So baking meringues on a rainy day isn't ideal. It's also a good idea to be aware of the environment within your kitchen since there can be moisture in the air from boiling water or from your dishwasher. Remember, the dryer the air, the crisper the meringue.

THE OTHER ENEMY IS FAT

Fat. Oil. Grease. Even a trace can prevent egg whites from whipping to their maximum volume and can also cause a whipped meringue to fall or deflate. You'd be surprised at the many sources: a tiny bit of egg yolk that's slipped into your egg whites, grease in your bowl or on your whisk, or even the natural oils on your hands. Make sure everything that touches your egg whites is squeaky clean and dry.

HOW TO CRACK EGGS

Start with eggs that are still cold from the refrigerator since the yolks are less likely to break when you're separating them from the whites. To crack the eggshell, tap it gently against a flat surface such as your kitchen counter (not against the edge of your mixing bowl) since this method is less likely to result in broken bits of shell mixed in with your egg whites. Then use your thumbs to pull the shell apart. If a bit of shell does make it into your egg white, use a larger piece of shell (rather than your fingers or a spoon) to scoop it out—for some crazy reason it acts like a magnet.

SEPARATING EGGS (OR AVOIDING SEPARATION ANXIETY)

A lot of people are intimidated by having to separate the whites from the yolks. Be brave. It's really not difficult once you get the hang of it. There are a number of different ways to separate eggs, so you may want to experiment a bit to find the one that's comfortable for you. The most important thing to remember is that none of the yolk—not even a speck—can infiltrate the egg whites, so it's good to have extra eggs on hand just in case of a mishap.

If you're wondering about the white stringy-looking part of the egg, it's called the "chalaza" and it's there to anchor the yolk to the white. The fresher the egg, the more prominent the chalaza, and since it doesn't interfere with the beating of the egg white, you don't need to remove it when making meringue.

To separate the egg white from the yolk, we like to use the "three bowl method." While adding a few extra dishes to wash, it saves you the heartache of having to toss out all your egg whites if a yolk breaks.

To start, set up two small glass or stainless steel bowls and the bowl of your electric stand mixer in your work area. (Never use plastic bowls since they can harbor grease or oil.)

Here's how it works:

Using one of the egg separating methods described below, let the egg white drip into bowl #1, then place the yolk into bowl #2. If you have an egg white with no bits of yolk in it in bowl #1, bask in the glory of a job well done, and pour that white into bowl #3—your mixing bowl. If, however, there is any bit of yolk in bowl #1, don't despair (it happens to the best of us); simply dispose of that egg white and start again in a clean, dry bowl. Repeat this process until your mixing bowl has all of the egg whites you need for your recipe and bowl #1 is empty.

Of course, if you have no plans for the egg yolks, you can just drop them down sink and make this a "two bowl method."

Here are some egg separating methods you can try:

SHELL TO SHELL: Crack the egg, and over a clean, dry bowl, carefully pour the egg yolk back and forth between the two shell halves while letting the egg white slip into the bowl beneath. This method can be a bit messy and you have to be very careful when using it so that the jagged edges of the shell don't tear the yolk.

HAND TO HAND: Empty the cracked egg into your hand and let the egg whites slip through your fingers into a clean, dry bowl. This is a fast, easy method; just make sure your hands are clean and dry so you don't transfer any of the natural oils in your skin to the egg whites.

COLANDER OR SLOTTED SPOON: Place a colander or large slotted spoon over a clean, dry bowl; crack eggs over the colander or slotted spoon and the whites will slide right into the bowl.

BRINGING EGGS TO ROOM TEMPERATURE

While eggs are easiest to separate when they're cold, egg whites achieve their maximum volume when beaten at room temperature. Bringing egg whites to room temperature will take about 30 minutes on your countertop. Or, if you want to speed things along, simply place your bowl of egg whites into a warm water bath for 2–3 minutes until they come to room temperature. Just make sure you don't get any water into the whites!

WHIPPING THE EGG WHITES

Starting slowly and then increasing the speed while beating your whites will maximize the volume.

ADDING THE SUGAR

When adding sugar, it's best to do so gradually, about 1 tablespoon at a time, waiting 5–10 seconds before adding the next spoonful. This will ensure that the sugar dissolves properly and that the egg whites reach their maximum volume. If you notice the sugar collecting along the sides of the mixing bowl, gently scrape down the sides with a clean rubber spatula and continue beating. When all the sugar is added and the meringue has formed stiff, glossy peaks, rub a dab between your index finger and thumb to make sure that all the sugar has dissolved. If it feels gritty, continue beating a bit. Just make sure not to overbeat!

Note: If the phone rings while you're in the middle of whipping your egg whites, you may want to let it go to voicemail. Stopping the process partway through, for more than a few seconds, may cause the meringue to deflate.

BAKING TEMPERATURE

Meringues are baked at a lower temperature than most other desserts. Many meringue recipes call for temperatures ranging from 250–300 degrees and a baking time anywhere from 30–45 minutes. This can yield a meringue that is crisp and fragile on the outside and moist and slightly chewy on the inside. Many Pavlova recipes call for baking the meringue at 350 degrees for a few minutes and then lowering the temperature for the remainder of the baking time. For cookies, we've found that the best results come from baking at an even lower temperature—200–225 degrees for a longer period of time and then turning off the oven and letting the meringues continue to dry and crisp in the oven for an additional hour or more. For recipes such as Classic French Meringues, this low temperature also allows the meringue to stay a snowy white rather than browning.

Note: Because ovens can be calibrated differently, through trial and error, you will find the best temperature for you.

STORING MERINGUES

Meringues (without any toppings) can be stored at room temperature in an airtight container for up to 5 days or in the freezer for up to 1 month. If stored meringues are chewy or sticky, bake at 200 degrees for about 10 minutes to restore their original crisp texture. Of course, recipes for meringues topped with perishable ingredients such as whipped cream should always be refrigerated.

Cookies

Crumbly, chewy, melt-in-your-mouth meringue cookies are the simplest of meringue desserts. In fact, there are barely any steps involved in the basic recipe—whipping some egg whites, perhaps with a bit of cream of tartar, and some sugar—what could be easier? They are gorgeous whether dropped from a spoon or piped with a star tip, and they always taste divine.

Meringue cookies are so low maintenance that they are sometimes called "Forgotten Cookies," because you can leave them in the oven to continue to crisp for hours after they have finished baking.

The sky is the limit in terms of flavor combinations for cookies, and we could have easily written an entire book of cookie recipes alone. If you are curious as to whether your favorite ingredients will translate to meringue, we encourage you to experiment. That's how we came up with our German Chocolate and Malted Milk Meringue recipes.

Chocolate–Chocolate Chip Clouds

Makes about 40

Crispy on the outside, but still a little bit gooey on the inside, these intensely chocolate meringues are incredibly popular with friends and family. Sometimes we'll substitute white chocolate chips to really shake things up.

3 large egg whites, room temperature
1/8 teaspoon cream of tartar
3/4 cup superfine sugar
2 tablespoons unsweetened cocoa powder
1/2 teaspoon pure vanilla extract
2/3 cup semisweet or milk chocolate chips

Preheat oven to 200 degrees.

In the bowl of an electric stand mixer fitted with the whisk attachment, beat egg whites and cream of tartar, increasing speed to medium-high until soft peaks form. Gradually add sugar, about a tablespoon at a time, beating on high until meringue has stiff, glossy peaks. Mix in cocoa powder and vanilla and then chocolate chips.

Drop by well-rounded teaspoons onto baking sheets lined with parchment paper, about 1 inch apart. Bake for 90 minutes. Turn off heat and leave meringues in the oven for 1 additional hour to crisp. Cool completely before removing from baking sheets.

Classic French Meringues

Makes about 48

On Linda's first visit to Paris, her Aunt Lola took her to a charming pâtisserie a short walk from her apartment. As Linda gazed at the array of magnificent meringues, she felt her heart racing. As soon as she returned to the States, she couldn't wait to try her hand at making them. This recipe is so divine; it's hard to believe there are only three ingredients.

4 large egg whites, room temperature
¼ teaspoon cream of tartar
1 cup superfine sugar

Preheat oven to 200 degrees.

In the bowl of an electric stand mixer fitted with the whisk attachment, beat egg whites and cream of tartar, increasing speed to medium-high until soft peaks form. Gradually add sugar, about a tablespoon at a time, beating on high until meringue has stiff, glossy peaks.

Drop by well-rounded teaspoons, or pipe through a pastry bag with a star or round tip, onto baking sheets lined with parchment paper, about 1 inch apart. Bake for 90 minutes. Turn off heat and leave meringues in the oven for 1 additional hour or more to crisp. Cool completely before removing from baking sheets.

Note: These classic cookies are included as an ingredient in several other recipes throughout this book.

Coconut Joys

Makes about 40

With a taste that's reminiscent of a Mounds bar, these little gems are crunchy on the outside and oh-so-chewy on the inside. You can also add chopped almonds because, as the old Almond Joy jingle goes, "sometimes you feel like a nut."

4 large egg whites, room temperature
1/4 teaspoon cream of tartar
1/2 cup superfine sugar
1/2 cup powdered sugar
1/2 teaspoon pure vanilla extract
3/4 cup sweetened shredded coconut
1 cup mini semisweet chocolate chips
1/2 cup chopped almonds, optional

Preheat oven to 200 degrees.

In the bowl of an electric stand mixer fitted with the whisk attachment, beat egg whites and cream of tartar, increasing speed to medium-high until soft peaks form. Add superfine sugar and then powdered sugar, about a tablespoon at a time. With a rubber spatula, very gently scrape down the sides of the mixing bowl because the powdered sugar is so lightweight it will fly up and stick to the sides of the bowl. Continue beating on high until peaks are stiff and glossy. Reduce to low and add vanilla, coconut, chocolate chips, and almonds; beat until combined.

Drop by well-rounded teaspoons onto baking sheets lined with parchment paper, about 1 inch apart. Bake for 90 minutes. Turn oven off and cool meringues in closed oven for 2 hours or until dry to the touch. Cool completely before removing from baking sheets.

Praline Meringues

Makes about 40

We've always had a soft spot for the delicious southern candy, Pralines, which are made with brown sugar and pecans. While praline candy can be temperamental and burn easily, these cookies always come out perfectly.

3 large egg whites, room temperature
Pinch of salt
1 cup lightly packed brown sugar
$^1/_2$ teaspoon pure vanilla extract
1 cup chopped pecans

Preheat oven to 200 degrees.

In the bowl of an electric stand mixer fitted with the whisk attachment, beat egg whites until foamy. Add salt and continue beating, increasing speed to medium-high, until soft peaks form. Gradually add brown sugar, about a tablespoon at a time, scraping down the sides of the bowl, as needed. Continue beating on high until meringue is glossy with stiff peaks. Add vanilla and pecans and beat just until combined.

Drop by well-rounded teaspoons onto parchment paper-lined baking sheets, about 1 inch apart. Bake for 90 minutes. Turn off heat and leave meringues in the oven for 1 additional hour or more to crisp. Cool completely before removing from baking sheets.

Brown Sugar Crisps

Makes about 100 small cookies

We shared a laugh when we discovered that as little girls, we both used to tiptoe into the kitchen to sneak spoonfuls of brown sugar when our mothers weren't looking. We still love it today, only now we don't have to tiptoe anywhere to get it. Brown sugar gives these cookies a lovely caramel flavor. And with just three ingredients, nothing could be simpler or more tempting.

2 large egg whites, room temperature
Small pinch of salt
1/2 cup firmly packed light brown sugar

Preheat oven to 200 degrees.

In the bowl of an electric stand mixer fitted with the whisk attachment, beat egg whites until foamy. Add salt and increase speed to medium-high; continue beating until soft peaks form. Lower speed and gradually add brown sugar, about a tablespoon at a time. Once all of the sugar has been added, scrape down the sides of the bowl with a rubber spatula to incorporate all of the sugar. Resume beating on high until meringue is glossy with stiff peaks.

Pipe with a decorative tip—we like to use a basketweave tip—onto parchment-lined baking sheets about 1/2 inch apart. Bake for 75 minutes. Turn oven off and leave the meringues in the oven for 1 additional hour or more to crisp. Cool completely before removing from baking sheets.

Lemon Twists

Makes about 40

Growing up in Southern California, Linda had a lemon tree in her yard. She would race outside to pick the lemons whenever she was able to cajole her mother into baking her lemon meringue pie. With both lemon juice and lemon zest, these cookies are reminiscent of a lemon meringue pie, only a lot simpler to make.

3 large egg whites, room temperature
1/4 teaspoon cream of tartar
1/8 teaspoon salt
3/4 cup superfine sugar
2 teaspoons freshly grated lemon zest, plus more for optional garnish
1/2 teaspoon fresh lemon juice
1/8 teaspoon pure vanilla extract

Preheat oven to 200 degrees.

In the bowl of an electric stand mixer fitted with the whisk attachment, beat egg whites and cream of tartar, increasing speed to medium-high until soft peaks form. Add salt then gradually add sugar, about a tablespoon at a time, beating on high until peaks are stiff and glossy. Add in lemon zest, lemon juice, and vanilla and beat until incorporated, about 1 minute more.

Pipe with a decorative tip onto baking sheets lined with parchment paper, about 1 inch apart. Sprinkle additional lemon zest on top of cookies, if desired. Bake for 90 minutes. Turn oven off and leave the cookies in the oven to dry, for about an hour. Cool completely before removing from baking sheets.

German Chocolate Cookies

Makes about 42

Pecans. Chocolate. Coconut. This combination can only mean one thing—German chocolate cake—or in this case, German chocolate meringue cookies.

3 large egg whites, room temperature
1/4 teaspoon cream of tartar
1/4 teaspoon salt
1 cup superfine sugar
2 tablespoons unsweetened cocoa powder
1/2 cup chopped pecans
1/2 cup miniature semisweet chocolate chips
1/2 cup sweetened shredded coconut

Preheat oven to 200 degrees.

In the bowl of an electric stand mixer fitted with the whisk attachment, beat egg whites and cream of tartar, increasing speed to medium-high until soft peaks form. Add salt then gradually add sugar, about a tablespoon at a time. Increase speed to high and beat until peaks are stiff and glossy. Beat in cocoa powder then fold in pecans, chocolate chips, and coconut.

Drop by well-rounded teaspoons onto baking sheets lined with parchment paper, about 1 inch apart. Bake for 90 minutes. Turn oven off, and leave meringues in closed oven up to 2 hours or until dry to the touch. Cool completely before removing from baking sheets.

Chocolate Mint Minis

Makes about 30

The first time we made these, we were a bit worried because the meringue had a strong mint aroma. But the mint flavor mellows during baking and they came out just right. We think they make the perfect after-dinner mint.

2 large egg whites, room temperature
$1/8$ teaspoon cream of tartar
$1/2$ cup superfine sugar
$1/2$ teaspoon pure vanilla extract
$3/4$ teaspoon peppermint extract
Green food coloring, optional
1 cup miniature semisweet chocolate chips

Preheat oven to 200 degrees.

In the bowl of an electric stand mixer fitted with the whisk attachment, beat egg whites and cream of tartar, increasing speed to medium-high until soft peaks form. Gradually add sugar, about a tablespoon at a time, beating on high until meringue is glossy with stiff peaks. Mix in extracts and food coloring, if using. Gently fold in the chocolate chips.

Drop by well-rounded teaspoons onto baking sheets lined with parchment paper, about 1 inch apart. Bake for 90 minutes. Turn off heat and leave the meringues in the oven to crisp, 1 hour or more. Cool completely before removing from baking sheets.

Coffee Cocoa Nib Delights

Makes about 40

When it comes to chocolate—the darker the better—at least in Jennifer's opinion, which is why she fell in love with cocoa nibs from the moment she tasted them. Pure roasted cocoa beans, the nibs have a crunchy, almost nutty consistency. Combined with coffee and the perfect amount of sugar, these make sublime cookies for grown-ups.

3 large egg whites
1/2 teaspoon cream of tartar
3/4 cup superfine sugar
2 tablespoons plus 1 teaspoon unsweetened cocoa powder, divided
2 teaspoons cocoa nibs*
1 teaspoon ground espresso or 2 teaspoons instant coffee granules
Dash of salt

Available in the baking aisle at specialty stores or supermarkets. You can substitute dark chocolate covered cocoa nibs if you'd like.

Preheat oven to 200 degrees.

In the bowl of an electric stand mixer fitted with the whisk attachment, beat egg whites and cream of tartar, increasing speed to medium-high until soft peaks form. Gradually add sugar, about a tablespoon at a time, beating on high until meringue is glossy with stiff peaks. Add 2 tablespoons cocoa powder, cocoa nibs, espresso, and salt. Beat just until incorporated.

Drop by well-rounded teaspoons or pipe with a decorative tip onto parchment-lined baking sheets, about 1 inch apart. Dust with remaining cocoa powder. Bake for 90 minutes. Turn oven off and leave the meringues in the oven to dry, 1 hour or more. Remove from oven and cool completely before removing from baking sheets.

Variation: For an additional chocolate kick, substitute 1 teaspoon crushed cocoa nibs for the 1 teaspoon unsweetened cocoa to dust cookies before baking.

Pistachio Meringues

Makes about 36

We love how the pistachios' earthy flavor provides a wonderful contrast to the sweetness of the meringue in these cookies.

1 1/4 cups shelled, dry roasted, unsalted pistachio nutmeat halves
1/2 cup powdered sugar
3 large egg whites, room temperature
1/4 teaspoon cream of tartar
2/3 cup superfine sugar
Green food coloring, optional

Preheat oven to 200 degrees.

In a small bowl, mix pistachio nuts and powdered sugar until the nuts are well coated. Set aside.

In the bowl of an electric stand mixer fitted with the whisk attachment, beat egg whites and cream of tartar, increasing speed to medium-high until soft peaks form. Gradually add superfine sugar, about a tablespoon at a time, beating on high until meringue is glossy with stiff peaks. Add food coloring, if using, and continue beating just until the color is well blended. Gently fold in nut mixture.

Drop by well-rounded teaspoons onto baking sheets lined with parchment paper, about 1 inch apart. Bake for 90 minutes. Turn off heat, and leave meringues in closed oven up to 2 hours. Cool completely before removing from baking sheets.

Chocolate Toffee Crunch Meringues

Makes about 40

Whenever Halloween comes around, Jennifer makes a pact with her son: she gets all of his Heath Bars in exchange for letting him trick or treat until after his bedtime. The sweet, salty crunch of toffee in these cookies satisfies the craving every time.

3 large egg whites, room temperature
1/4 teaspoon cream of tartar
Pinch of salt
1 cup superfine sugar
3 tablespoons unsweetened cocoa powder
1/2 teaspoon pure vanilla extract
1/3 cup miniature semisweet chocolate chips
1/3 cup English toffee bits (such as Heath)

Preheat oven to 200 degrees.

In the bowl of an electric stand mixer fitted with the whisk attachment, beat egg whites and cream of tartar, increasing speed to medium-high until soft peaks form. Add salt then gradually add the sugar, about a tablespoon at a time, beating on high until meringue is glossy with stiff peaks. Beat in cocoa powder and vanilla. Fold in chocolate chips and toffee bits.

Drop by well-rounded teaspoons onto baking sheets lined with parchment paper, about 1 inch apart. Bake for 90 minutes. Turn off heat and leave the meringues in the oven to dry, 1 hour or longer. Cool completely before removing from baking sheets.

Chocolate-Dipped Almond Meringues

Makes about 24

These voluminous almond cookies look so elegant dipped in chocolate and topped with whole almonds. Chocolate and almond—what a classic combination.

4 large egg whites, room temperature
Pinch of cream of tartar
1/4 teaspoon salt
1 cup superfine sugar
1/4 teaspoon almond extract
1/2 cup tempered chocolate pieces, or semisweet chocolate chips, tempered*
24 whole almonds

Preheat oven to 200 degrees.

In the bowl of an electric stand mixer fitted with the whisk attachment, beat egg whites and cream of tartar, increasing speed to medium-high until soft peaks form. Add salt then gradually add sugar, about a tablespoon at a time, beating on high until stiff peaks form. Gently mix in almond extract.

Drop meringue by rounded tablespoons or pipe with a decorative tip onto parchment-lined baking sheets. Bake for 2 hours or until dry. Turn oven off; leave meringues in oven 1 hour or more until crisp. Cool completely before removing from baking sheets.

Prepare chocolate coating, tempering it if you are not serving the cookies right away so that the chocolate remains smooth and shiny. Otherwise, you can melt the chocolate in the microwave at 30 second intervals, being careful not to burn it. Dip top half of each meringue in chocolate, top with an almond and place on wire rack to dry.

*To temper chocolate: Melt chocolate in a double boiler to about 115 degrees. Let it cool to around 80 degrees, while stirring. Put chocolate back over heat until temperature is 90 degrees (check with manufacturer about your particular kind of chocolate, as it can vary by a degree or two) and use as instructed.

Variation: For a different look, you can substitute slivered or chopped almonds for the whole almonds.

Cinnamon Stars

Makes about 40

We loved making Snickerdoodles with our mothers when we were young, especially the part where we rolled the balls of dough into the cinnamon-sugar mixture. Now our children love making this elegant cinnamon meringue with us.

3 large egg whites, room temperature
1/4 teaspoon cream of tartar
1/8 teaspoon salt
3/4 cup superfine sugar
1 tablespoon packed dark brown sugar
1/2 teaspoon pure vanilla extract
1 teaspoon cinnamon

Preheat oven to 200 degrees.

In the bowl of an electric stand mixer fitted with the whisk attachment, beat egg whites and cream of tartar, increasing speed to medium-high until soft peaks form. Beat in salt then gradually add the sugars, about a tablespoon at a time, beating on high until meringue has stiff, glossy peaks. Add the vanilla and cinnamon and beat until incorporated, about 1 minute more.

Spoon the meringue into a pastry bag fitted with a large star tip. Pipe meringue stars onto baking sheets lined with parchment paper, about 1 inch apart. Bake for 90 minutes. Turn off heat and leave the meringues in the oven to dry, 1 hour or more. Cool completely before removing from baking sheets.

Malted Milk Meringues

Makes about 48

One of our favorite indulgences is a thick chocolate malted milkshake, so this cookie was created as a tribute. In our first attempt at developing the recipe, we added malt powder, and watched in horror as it deflated the meringue. So we scratched that off the ingredient list. The malt balls didn't have the same affect and they practically disappear into the cookies for a subtle malt flavor. (By the way, malt contains gluten, so if you're on a gluten-free diet you're out of luck.)

3 large egg whites, room temperature
1/8 teaspoon cream of tartar
1 cup superfine sugar
2 tablespoons unsweetened cocoa powder
1/2 teaspoon pure vanilla extract
6 ounces high quality malt balls, coarsely chopped

Preheat oven to 200 degrees.

In the bowl of an electric stand mixer fitted with the whisk attachment, beat egg whites and cream of tartar, increasing speed to medium-high until soft peaks form. Gradually add sugar, about a tablespoon at a time, beating on high until peaks are stiff and glossy. Mix in cocoa powder and vanilla, about 1 minute more. Gently fold in malt balls.

Drop by well-rounded teaspoons onto parchment-lined baking sheets, about 1 inch apart. Bake for 90 minutes. Turn off heat and leave the meringues in the oven to dry, 1 hour or more. Cool completely before removing from baking sheets.

Nocciola Baci

Makes about 16 sandwich cookies

Leave it to the Italians to create something as decadent as Baci—chocolate kisses filled with hazelnut cream and a hazelnut center. As an homage to this Perugian treat, we created these delicious meringue cookies. Hazelnut meringue on one side and chocolate-hazelnut meringue on the other, these sandwich cookies are held together with a creamy layer of Chocolate-Hazelnut Filling. *Bellissimo!*

MERINGUES
1 1/2 cups (about 6.75 ounces) blanched, chopped hazelnuts
2 large egg whites, room temperature
1/8 teaspoon cream of tartar
1/8 teaspoon salt
3/4 cup superfine sugar

1/4 cup powdered sugar
1 tablespoon unsweetened cocoa powder

CHOCOLATE-HAZELNUT FILLING
1/3 cup chocolate-hazelnut spread (such as Nutella), room temperature
1/2 tablespoon sifted powdered sugar

MERINGUES: Preheat oven to 200 degrees.

In a food processor, pulse hazelnuts until finely ground. Set aside.

In the bowl of an electric stand mixer fitted with the whisk attachment, beat egg whites and cream of tartar, increasing speed to medium-high until soft peaks form. Add salt then gradually add superfine sugar, followed by powdered sugar, about a tablespoon at a time, beating on high until peaks are stiff and glossy. Add hazelnuts and mix just until incorporated.

With a rubber spatula, divide the meringue mixture roughly in half in the mixing bowl. Use half of the mixture to make plain hazelnut cookies by dropping well-rounded teaspoons onto a parchment-lined baking sheet, about 1 inch apart. Add the cocoa powder to the remaining meringue mixture and beat just until combined. Drop by well-rounded teaspoons onto another parchment-lined baking sheet. Bake for 90 minutes. Remove from the oven immediately so that the cookies will remain a little bit chewy in the center. Cool completely before removing from baking sheets.

CHOCOLATE-HAZELNUT FILLING: In a small bowl, mix the chocolate-hazelnut spread and powdered sugar until incorporated.

TO ASSEMBLE BACI COOKIES: Gently spread about 1/2 teaspoon of the Chocolate-Hazelnut Filling onto the bottom (flat side) of one chocolate-hazelnut cookie then place the flat side of a hazelnut cookie on top, gently pressing the two together. Repeat with the remaining cookies and filling. Enjoy immediately, or store in an airtight container with pieces of wax paper separating the layers of cookies.

Alfajores Con Baño Blanco

Makes about 22–24 sandwich cookies

On a trip to Buenos Aires several years ago, Linda was delighted to discover so many wonderful desserts made with dulce de leche, the addictive caramel-like spread. One of the most memorable was alfajores, shortbread cookies filled with dulce de leche. These delicious cookies are coated with a crispy white baño blanco (Spanish for "white bath"), made using the Italian meringue method of adding a hot sugar syrup to beaten egg whites.

ALFAJORES COOKIES
2 cups sifted flour
¼ cup sifted powdered sugar
½ teaspoon salt
1 cup (2 sticks) unsalted butter, softened, cut into 1 tablespoon-size pieces
1½ cups dulce de leche, room temperature
  (from a 13.4 ounce can or a jar of store-bought dulce de leche)

BAÑO BLANCO MERINGUE
1 cup sugar
¼ cup water
2 large egg whites, room temperature

ALFAJORES COOKIES: Preheat oven to 350 degrees.

In the bowl of an electric stand mixer, beat flour, sugar, salt, and butter on medium speed until the dough comes together. Form the dough into a ball, cover in plastic wrap, and refrigerate for 20–30 minutes.

Sprinkle some flour onto your work surface and, with a rolling pin, roll the dough ⅛-inch thick. Cut circles, using a 2-inch round cookie cutter, and transfer to parchment paper-lined baking sheets. Bring the dough scraps together and gently press into a ball. Flour your work surface again and re-roll the dough to ⅛-inch thick and cut out more circles. (You should end up with between 44 and 48 circles.)

Bake the cookies until they are golden and firm, about 15–20 minutes. Remove from the oven and let cool for 5 minutes before transferring to a wire rack to cool completely, about 30 minutes more.

Spread about 1 teaspoon of dulce de leche on the flat side of a cookie and top with the flat side of another cookie. Continue until all of your sandwich cookies have been formed. Set aside.

BAÑO BLANCO MERINGUE: Place sugar in a small saucepan then cover with water. Heat on medium, tilting and swirling the pan occasionally, but do not stir. In the meantime, start beating the egg whites—instructions

Alfajores Con Baño Blanco (continued)

below. When all the sugar has dissolved, increase heat to medium-high and boil until the sugar syrup reaches 235 degrees (soft ball stage) on a candy thermometer. Immediately remove from heat.

In the bowl of an electric stand mixer fitted with the whisk attachment, beat the egg whites on medium-high speed until they form soft peaks. Slowly drizzle the sugar syrup into the bowl with the egg whites. Continue beating until the meringue is glossy but not stiff.

One by one, use a pastry brush to "paint" the baño blanco meringue on the tops and sides of the dulce de leche-filled cookies. Transfer to a baking sheet lined with wax paper. Let cookies dry for several hours or overnight so that the baño blanco forms a crust on the outside of the Alfajores. Store in an airtight container with the cookies separated by wax paper.

Meringue Mushrooms

Meringue can be piped into a variety of shapes, but we particularly love the whimsical meringue "mushrooms" used to garnish a Bûche de Noël, the classic French Christmas cake, which looks like a Yule log (page 201).

2 large egg whites, room temperature
1/8 teaspoon cream of tartar
1/2 cup superfine sugar
1/4 teaspoon pure vanilla extract
Sifted unsweetened cocoa powder

Preheat oven to 200 degrees and line 2 baking sheets with parchment paper.

In the bowl of an electric stand mixer fitted with the whisk attachment, beat egg whites and cream of tartar, increasing speed to medium-high until soft peaks form. Gradually add sugar, about a tablespoon at a time, beating on high until peaks are stiff and glossy. Beat in vanilla.

Transfer meringue to a pastry bag fitted with a 1/2-inch plain round tip. Form 12 mushroom caps by piping 1 1/2-inch smooth, round mounds onto one of the prepared baking sheets. Dust with cocoa powder. On the other baking sheet, form stems by piping 12 pointed cones, approximately 1 1/4 inches high, starting about 1/4 inch above the baking sheet and pulling the pastry bag straight up while squeezing and applying even pressure. The stems will be flat on the bottom and pointed at the top. (Save the remaining meringue in the refrigerator to use to secure the meringue mushroom stems to the caps.) Bake caps and stems for 90 minutes. Turn off heat and leave meringues in the oven for 1 additional hour or more to continue drying. Cool completely before removing from baking sheets.

With the tip of a small sharp knife, carefully poke a small hole in the center of the flat underside of each meringue mushroom cap. Pipe a small dab of meringue into each cap then gently insert the pointed end of the stems. Store them upside down or on their sides in an airtight container for up to a week.

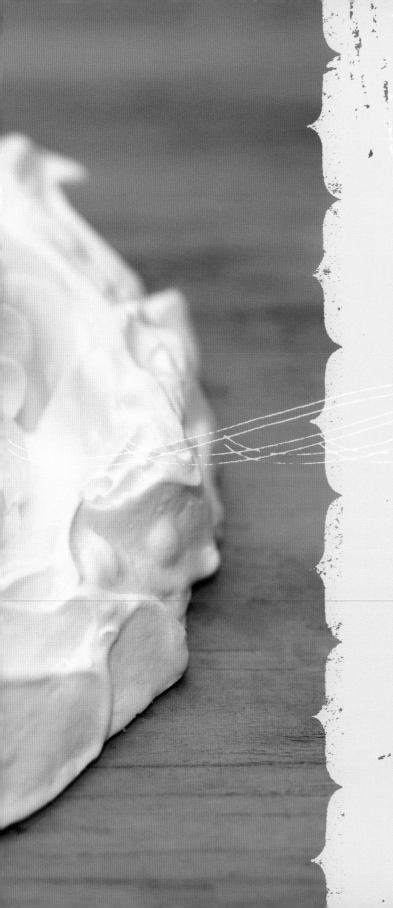

Pavlovas

Pavlova is a gorgeous meringue dessert that resembles a cloud topped with whipped cream and fruit, and always elicits oohs and ahhs when presented. Originally created in honor of the Russian ballerina Anna Pavlova during her tour down under in the 1920s, both Australia and New Zealand claim Pavlova as their own. We'll leave that for the U.N. to sort out, but we can all agree that Pavlova is an elegant, exquisite meringue dessert.

Pavlovas can be formed either by piping the meringue in a circle with higher sides or by using a spoon to spread the meringue to form the shell. Either way, it will be beautiful. With any of the recipes in this chapter, you can make one large Pavlova, which you will slice into individual servings, or create multiple individual serving-size mini-Pavlovas. For mini-Pavlovas, simply pipe 8 (4-inch) meringues and shorten the baking time by approximately 15 minutes. Regardless of the size, it's best to add the whipped cream and fruit just before serving so that the Pavlova shell stays crisp.

Chocolate Angel "Pie"

Serves 8

Who says that chocolate can't be decadently rich and light at the same time? This gorgeous dessert is part Pavlova and part pie, but with just one bite, you'll know that it's all heaven.

MERINGUE PIE SHELL
2 large egg whites, room temperature
1/8 teaspoon cream of tartar
Pinch of salt
1/2 cup superfine sugar
1 teaspoon pure vanilla extract

FILLING
2 cups heavy whipping cream
1 1/4 cups powdered sugar
1/2 cup unsweetened cocoa powder
1 teaspoon instant espresso or 2 teaspoons instant coffee granules
1 1/2 teaspoons pure vanilla extract
1 tablespoon milk

MERINGUE PIE SHELL: Preheat oven to 300 degrees. Spray a 9-inch metal pie pan with a flour-based cooking spray.

In the bowl of an electric stand mixer fitted with the whisk attachment, beat egg whites and cream of tartar on medium-high speed until soft peaks form. Beat in salt then add sugar, about a tablespoon at a time, beating on high until peaks are stiff and glossy. Add vanilla and beat until incorporated.

With a rubber spatula, evenly spread meringue over bottom and up sides of pie pan. Bake 1 hour. Turn off oven and let meringue remain in oven 1 additional hour to crisp. Remove from oven and cool meringue shell in pie pan on wire rack.

FILLING: In a large bowl with electric mixer at medium speed, beat whipping cream and sugar until it starts to thicken. Add cocoa powder, dissolved espresso (1 teaspoon espresso in 1 teaspoon hot water), and vanilla and beat until thoroughly blended and cream is stiff; do not over beat. Beat in milk.

TO ASSEMBLE AND GARNISH PIE: With rubber spatula, spread chocolate cream into cooled meringue shell. Garnish with a dusting of more powdered sugar or cocoa powder, or with chocolate curls. Refrigerate for 2 hours, uncovered, before serving.

Chocolate Raspberry Mini-Pavlovas

Makes 12

Imagine what a chocolate cloud would taste like, then add chantilly cream, raspberries, and of course, more chocolate. Decadent and delicious.

CHOCOLATE PAVLOVA SHELLS
8 large egg whites, room temperature
2 teaspoons white wine vinegar
Pinch of salt
1 1/2 cups superfine sugar
1 teaspoon pure vanilla extract
4 teaspoons cornstarch
2 tablespoons unsweetened cocoa powder

CHANTILLY CREAM
3 cups heavy whipping cream
4 tablespoons sugar
1 teaspoon pure vanilla extract

TOPPING AND GARNISH
3 pints fresh raspberries, rinsed and dried
Chocolate shavings (take a chocolate bar and "peel" chocolate with vegetable peeler)

CHOCOLATE PAVLOVA SHELLS: Preheat oven to 350 degrees.

In the bowl of an electric stand mixer fitted with the whisk attachment, beat egg whites until foamy. Add vinegar and salt and beat on medium-high until you have soft peaks. Slowly add sugar, about a tablespoon at a time, beating on high until whites are stiff and shiny. Add vanilla then sprinkle cornstarch and cocoa powder over egg whites; beat just until incorporated.

Draw 12 (4-inch) circles on parchment paper with pencil; turn paper over. Spoon or pipe meringue into circles on marked paper, making sides higher than center. Place in oven and immediately turn heat down to 300 degrees. Bake 30 minutes, and then turn oven off and leave meringues in for 30 more minutes. Take out of oven and let cool. When completely cooled, remove meringues by gently peeling them off the parchment or by sliding an offset spatula or knife underneath the shells.

CHANTILLY CREAM: With an electric mixer, whip cream, sugar, and vanilla until stiff.

TO ASSEMBLE PAVLOVAS: When ready to serve, place Pavlovas on individual serving plates and spoon Chantilly Cream into meringue shells. Top with berries and sprinkle chocolate shavings over the top.

Chocolate-Flecked Pavlova with Chocolate Mascarpone and Strawberries

Serves 8

Mascarpone is a smooth, creamy cheese used in a variety of sweet and savory dishes in the Lombardy region of Italy. Here we've mixed it with two different kinds of chocolate for a delicious change of pace from the whipped cream filling in most Pavlovas.

PAVLOVA SHELL
1 cup superfine sugar
1 teaspoon cornstarch
4 large egg whites, room temperature
1 teaspoon vinegar
Pinch of salt
1/3 cup chopped bittersweet chocolate

CHOCOLATE MASCARPONE FILLING
2 ounces semisweet chocolate
8 ounces mascarpone cheese, room temperature
1/4 cup sifted powdered sugar
1 1/2 teaspoons sifted unsweetened cocoa powder
1/2 teaspoon pure vanilla extract

STRAWBERRIES
4 cups fresh strawberries, rinsed, dried, hulled, and sliced in half
1 tablespoon sugar, or more to taste

PAVLOVA SHELL: Preheat oven to 350 degrees. In a small bowl, whisk together sugar and cornstarch; set aside.

In the bowl of an electric stand mixer fitted with the whisk attachment, beat egg whites until foamy. Add vinegar and salt and increase speed to medium-high, beating until soft peaks form. Beat in sugar mixture on high, about a tablespoon at a time, until all the mixture is incorporated and peaks are glossy and stiff. Fold in chocolate.

Line a baking sheet with parchment paper. Pipe or spoon meringue into a 10-inch circle, making sides higher than center. Bake for 5 minutes, then lower the temperature to 250 degrees and continue baking for 1 hour. Turn the heat off but leave the meringue shell in the oven for 3 hours or more (or overnight) so that it continues to dry. When completely cooled, loosen the meringue by gently peeling it off the parchment or by sliding an offset spatula or knife underneath the shell.

CHOCOLATE MASCARPONE FILLING: Heat the chocolate in a small bowl in the microwave, in 30-second intervals, until melted; set aside. In a medium bowl, combine the mascarpone, sugar, cocoa powder, and vanilla. Fold the melted chocolate into the mascarpone mixture until blended and smooth.

STRAWBERRIES: Just before you're ready to serve the Pavlova, toss strawberries with sugar in a medium bowl.

TO ASSEMBLE PAVLOVA: Place meringue shell on a serving plate. Fill the center with the chocolate mascarpone and top with strawberries in concentric circles or pile the berries on top for a less formal look.

Brown Sugar Plum Pavlova

Serves 8

The caramel flavor of the brown sugar and the maple syrup-sweetened whipped cream make the perfect backdrop for luscious plums. The brown sugar plum fairy would be proud.

PAVLOVA SHELL
4 large egg whites, room temperature
Pinch of salt
1 teaspoon apple cider vinegar
1/3 cup firmly packed brown sugar
2/3 cup superfine sugar
1 teaspoon cornstarch

PLUMS
2/3 cup firmly packed brown sugar
1/2 cup water
Pinch of salt
6 fresh plums, skin on, halved, pitted, and cut into
    8 slices each (about 3 cups of fruit)
Tiny pinch of ground cloves

MAPLE WHIPPED CREAM
1 cup heavy whipping cream
2 tablespoons pure maple syrup

PAVLOVA SHELL: Preheat oven to 350 degrees.

In the bowl of an electric stand mixer fitted with the whisk attachment, beat egg whites until foamy. Increase speed to medium-high and add salt and vinegar, beating until soft peaks form. Starting with the brown sugar, add the sugars about a tablespoon at a time, until all of the sugar is incorporated. Stop the mixer to scrape down the sides of the bowl. Continue beating on high until meringue has stiff, glossy peaks. Beat in cornstarch, about 1 minute more.

Line a baking sheet with parchment paper. Pipe or spoon meringue into a 10-inch circle, making sides higher than center. Bake for 5 minutes, then lower the temperature to 250 degrees and continue baking for 1 hour. Turn the heat off but leave the meringue shell in the oven for 3 hours or more (or overnight) so that it continues to dry. When completely cooled, loosen the meringue by gently peeling it off the parchment or by sliding an offset spatula or knife underneath the shell.

PLUMS: In a nonreactive skillet, bring sugar and water to a boil over medium heat; stir continually until sugar is dissolved. Boil the sugar syrup for 3 minutes then add salt, plums, and cloves. Return to boil, gently stirring so that the plums are coated on all sides. Cook for 3–4 minutes, until tender. Remove from heat to cool while you make whipped cream.

MAPLE WHIPPED CREAM: With an electric mixer, beat cream and syrup until stiff.

TO ASSEMBLE PAVLOVA: Place meringue shell on serving plate. Fill with whipped cream and top with plums; drizzle with about 1 tablespoon of the plum syrup.

Pavlova with Balsamic Strawberries

Serves 8

The first time Jennifer tasted strawberries macerated in balsamic vinegar in Italy, she was astounded at how much the vinegar brought out the flavor of the sweet summer berries. While it's a very sophisticated flavor combination, we have yet to meet anyone who doesn't love it.

PAVLOVA SHELL
4 large egg whites, room temperature
1 teaspoon white wine vinegar
Pinch of salt
3/4 cup superfine sugar
1/2 teaspoon pure vanilla extract
2 teaspoons cornstarch

WHIPPED CREAM
1 1/2 cups heavy whipping cream
2 tablespoons sugar
1/2 teaspoon almond extract

STRAWBERRIES
2 cups fresh strawberries, hulled and sliced
3 tablespoons sugar
2 to 3 tablespoons balsamic vinegar
Powdered sugar, for garnish

PAVLOVA SHELL: Preheat oven to 350 degrees.

In the bowl of an electric stand mixer fitted with the whisk attachment, beat egg whites until foamy. Add vinegar and salt and beat on medium-high until soft peaks form. Slowly add sugar, about a tablespoon at a time, beating on high until meringue is stiff and shiny. Add vanilla then sift cornstarch over whites and beat until incorporated.

Line a baking sheet with parchment paper. Pipe meringue into a 10-inch circle, making sides higher than center. Or, using the back of a spoon, spread the meringue from the center out to the sides to form a 10-inch shell. Place in oven and turn heat down immediately to 300 degrees. Bake 45 minutes and then turn oven off, but leave the shell in the oven for an additional 30–40 minutes until dry and slightly crispy. Take out of the oven to cool. When completely cooled, remove meringue by gently peeling it off the parchment or by sliding an offset spatula or knife underneath the shell.

WHIPPED CREAM: With an electric mixer, whip cream with sugar and almond extract until stiff.

STRAWBERRIES: Combine strawberries, sugar, and vinegar in a medium bowl. Stir and let macerate for 30 minutes or until ready to use.

TO ASSEMBLE PAVLOVA: Spoon whipped cream into meringue shell and top with balsamic macerated strawberries. Dust with powdered sugar just before serving.

Banana Cream Pavlova

Serves 8

Jennifer's Grammy Olga was a cream pie fanatic, and it was she who first introduced Jen to banana cream pie. Inspired by this memory, we created a Pavlova with warm caramelized bananas, and we couldn't resist adding walnuts and shaved chocolate. Grammy would be proud.

PAVLOVA SHELL
4 large egg whites, room temperature (reserve 3 egg yolks for custard)
1 teaspoon white wine vinegar
Pinch of salt
1 cup superfine sugar
1 teaspoon pure vanilla extract
2 teaspoons cornstarch

CUSTARD FILLING
3 large egg yolks, room temperature
6 tablespoons flour
1 cup sugar
$1/4$ teaspoon salt
2 cups scalded milk
4 tablespoons unsalted butter, cut into $1/4$-inch slices, room temperature
2 teaspoons pure vanilla extract

CARAMELIZED BANANAS
2 tablespoons unsalted butter
4 firm, but ripe bananas, sliced into $1/4$-inch rounds
2 tablespoons firmly packed brown sugar

TOPPINGS AND GARNISH
1 cup chopped walnuts, or more, to taste
Chocolate shavings
$1/2$ cup graham cracker crumbs, optional

PAVLOVA SHELL: Preheat oven to 350 degrees.

In the bowl of an electric stand mixer fitted with the whisk attachment, beat egg whites until foamy; add vinegar and salt and beat on medium-high to soft peaks. Slowly add sugar, about a tablespoon at time, beating on high until whites are stiff and shiny. Add vanilla then sprinkle cornstarch over whites and beat just until incorporated.

Banana Cream Pavlova (continued)

On a baking sheet lined with parchment paper, pipe or spoon meringue into a 10-inch circle, making sides higher than the center. Place in oven and turn heat down immediately to 300 degrees. Bake 1 hour and then turn oven off, leaving Pavlova in for an additional hour. Take out of the oven and cool. When completely cooled, remove meringue by gently peeling it off the parchment or by sliding an offset spatula or knife underneath the shell.

CUSTARD FILLING: Lightly beat egg yolks in a small bowl; set aside.

In a heavy saucepan, combine flour, sugar, and salt. Gradually stir in milk; continue stirring until smooth. Over medium heat, bring mixture to a boil, stirring constantly. Boil for 1 minute, stirring the entire time, then remove pan from heat. Add $1/4$ cup of the hot milk mixture to the beaten egg yolks, a little at a time, whisking constantly. Stir the tempered egg mixture back into the pan of hot milk. Cook over medium heat, stirring constantly, until the custard is very thick, about 3 minutes. Remove pan from heat and stir in the butter, 1 slice at a time, followed by vanilla, and stir until smooth. Cover the entire surface with plastic wrap to prevent the custard from forming a skin and chill in refrigerator until ready to fill Pavlova shell.

CARAMELIZED BANANAS: In a sauté pan over medium heat, melt butter and then add banana slices. Sprinkle brown sugar over the top and cook, stirring to coat, until the bananas are caramelized, about 2 minutes.

TO ASSEMBLE PAVLOVA: Transfer Pavlova shell to serving plate. Fill shell with custard, and then top with warm caramelized bananas, walnuts, chocolate shavings, and graham cracker crumbs, if using. Serve immediately.

Cherries Jubilee Mini-Pavlovas

Makes 8

Cherries Jubilee, a classic 1950s recipe of flambéed canned cherries over ice cream, is making a comeback. We decided to update the old version with fresh cherries and serve it atop a meringue shell to create a new classic: Cherries Jubilee Pavlova. Be sure to call your guests to the kitchen before you flambé the cherries—it adds a bit of drama to the presentation.

PAVLOVA SHELLS
4 large egg whites, room temperature
1 teaspoon white wine vinegar
Pinch of salt
3/4 cup superfine sugar
1/2 teaspoon pure vanilla extract
2 teaspoons cornstarch

FILLING
1 quart high quality vanilla ice cream

CHERRIES JUBILEE TOPPING
4 tablespoons unsalted butter
1/4 cup sugar
1 pound fresh Bing cherries, pitted
1 teaspoon orange zest
1/4 cup cognac

PAVLOVA SHELLS: Preheat oven to 350 degrees.

In the bowl of an electric stand mixer fitted with the whisk attachment, beat egg whites until foamy. Increase speed to medium-high and add vinegar and salt; continue beating to soft peaks. Slowly add sugar, about a tablespoon at a time, beating on high until whites are stiff and shiny. Add vanilla then sprinkle cornstarch over whites and beat just until incorporated.

Line a baking sheet with parchment paper. Pipe meringue into 8 (4-inch) circles, making sides higher than center. Place in oven and turn heat down immediately to 300 degrees. Bake 30 minutes and then turn oven off, but leave shells in for an additional 30 minutes until dry and slightly crispy. Take out of the oven to cool. When completely cooled, remove meringues by gently peeling them off the parchment or by sliding an offset spatula or knife underneath the shells.

CHERRIES JUBILEE TOPPING: In a large skillet, melt butter over medium heat then add sugar, cherries, and zest. Stir for about 5–6 minutes, until cherries become soft and sugar is completely dissolved. Turn off heat. Add cognac and ignite with a long lighter, being careful not to burn yourself! Let the flame die out. Keep cherries warm in their sauce, or if necessary, warm just before serving.

TO ASSEMBLE PAVLOVAS: When ready to serve, place Pavlovas on individual serving plates, put a scoop of vanilla ice cream into the center of each Pavlova, and spoon warm cherries and sauce over the top.

Lemon Mini-Pavlovas with Lemon Curd Whipped Cream and Blueberries

Makes 12

Lemon and blueberries are a wonderful flavor combination, and this Pavlova with its whipped cream-lightened lemon curd filling makes a lovely light summer dessert.

PAVLOVA SHELLS
8 large egg whites, room temperature
   (save 2 yolks for curd)
2 teaspoons white wine vinegar
Pinch of salt
1 1/2 cups superfine sugar
1 teaspoon pure vanilla extract
1 teaspoon lemon zest
4 teaspoons cornstarch

LEMON CURD
2 large eggs
2 large egg yolks

3/4 cup sugar
Zest of 1 to 2 lemons (about 1 tablespoon)
1/3 cup lemon juice
1/2 cup (1 stick) unsalted butter, cut into pieces

WHIPPED CREAM
1 1/2 cups heavy whipping cream
1 tablespoon sugar

BLUEBERRY TOPPING
3 pints fresh blueberries, rinsed and dried
Powdered sugar, optional

PAVLOVA SHELLS: Preheat oven to 350 degrees.

Line 2 baking sheets with parchment paper. Draw 12 (4-inch) circles onto paper; turn paper over. You should be able to see the circles.

In the bowl of an electric stand mixer fitted with the whisk attachment, beat egg whites until foamy. Add vinegar and salt and beat on medium-high until you have soft peaks. Slowly add sugar, about a tablespoon at a time, and beat on high until stiff and shiny. Add vanilla and lemon zest then sprinkle cornstarch over meringue and beat until incorporated.

Pipe meringue into circles on marked paper, making sides higher than center. Place in oven and turn heat down immediately to 300 degrees. Bake 30 minutes then turn oven off, leaving Pavlovas in oven for additional 30 minutes. Take out of oven to cool. When completely cooled, remove meringues by gently peeling them off the parchment or by sliding an offset spatula or knife underneath the shells.

LEMON CURD: Combine all ingredients in double boiler. Whisk frequently until thick. Strain and refrigerate.

WHIPPED CREAM: With an electric mixer, whip cream and sugar together until stiff.

TO ASSEMBLE AND SERVE PAVLOVAS: When lemon curd is cold, fold into whipped cream. You now have a light, fluffy lemon whipped cream. Place meringues on individual dessert plates and fill with lemon cream. Top with blueberries and dust with powdered sugar, if desired.

Kiwi Pavlova with Lime Zest

Serves 8

Kiwi and lime is a great flavor combination, but when you add fresh mint and sugar, it really kicks it up a notch. We stopped short of calling this a mojito Pavlova, but if you want to add rum, we won't tell.

PAVLOVA SHELL
4 large egg whites, room temperature
1 teaspoon white wine vinegar
Pinch of salt
3/4 cup superfine sugar
1 teaspoon pure vanilla extract
Zest of 2 limes (about 1 tablespoon)
2 teaspoons cornstarch

WHIPPED CREAM
1 cup heavy whipping cream
2 tablespoons sugar

KIWI TOPPING
6 fresh kiwis, peeled and sliced
Juice of 1 lime
1 to 2 tablespoons superfine sugar
1 heaping tablespoon chopped fresh mint
Drizzle of rum, optional, for you mojito people

PAVLOVA SHELL: Preheat oven to 350 degrees.

In the bowl of an electric stand mixer fitted with the whisk attachment, beat egg whites until foamy. Add vinegar and salt and beat on medium-high to soft peaks. Slowly add sugar, about a tablespoon at a time, beating on high until whites are stiff and shiny. Add vanilla and lime zest then sprinkle cornstarch over whites and beat until incorporated.

On a parchment paper-lined baking sheet, pipe or spoon meringue into a 10-inch circle, making sides higher than the center. Place in oven and turn heat down immediately to 300 degrees. Bake 45 minutes and then turn oven off, leaving meringue in for an additional 40 minutes, or until crisp. Take out of the oven and cool. When completely cooled, remove meringue by gently peeling it off the parchment or by sliding an offset spatula or knife underneath the shell.

WHIPPED CREAM: With an electric mixer, whip cream and sugar until you have stiff peaks. Chill until ready to use.

KIWI TOPPING: Place sliced kiwis in a medium bowl. Add lime juice, sugar, mint, and rum, if using, and gently toss. Let macerate for 30 minutes, or up to 24 hours.

TO ASSEMBLE PAVLOVA: Fill Pavlova shell with whipped cream and top with macerated kiwis.

Classic Berry Pavlova

Serves 8

Fresh, juicy berries atop luscious whipped cream and a lighter-than-air meringue shell. No matter how great the dinner, this show-stopping dessert will be what your guests talk about for days to come.

MERINGUE SHELL
4 large egg whites, room temperature
1 teaspoon white vinegar
Pinch of salt
1 cup superfine sugar
1 teaspoon cornstarch

WHIPPED CREAM FILLING
1 cup heavy whipping cream

3 tablespoons powdered sugar
1 tablespoon pure vanilla extract

BERRIES
4 cups fresh berries, any combination of sliced strawberries, raspberries, and blueberries
1 to 2 tablespoons sugar, optional

MERINGUE SHELL: Preheat oven to 350 degrees.

In the bowl of an electric stand mixer fitted with the whisk attachment, beat egg whites until foamy. Add vinegar and salt and beat on medium-high until soft peaks form. Add sugar, about a tablespoon at a time, beating until all of the sugar is incorporated. Continue beating on high until meringue is stiff with glossy peaks. Beat in cornstarch, about 1 minute more.

Line a baking sheet with parchment paper. Pipe or spoon meringue into a 10-inch circle, making sides higher than center. Bake for 5 minutes then lower the temperature to 250 degrees and continue baking for 1 hour. Turn the heat off but leave the meringue shell in the oven for 3 hours or more (or overnight) so that it continues to dry. When completely cooled, loosen the meringue by gently peeling it off the parchment or by sliding an offset spatula or knife underneath the shell.

WHIPPED CREAM FILLING: With an electric mixer, whip cream, sugar, and vanilla until stiff.

BERRIES: Rinse the berries and allow to dry on paper towels. Transfer to a mixing bowl and toss with sugar.

TO ASSEMBLE PAVLOVA: Gently transfer the meringue shell to your serving plate. Spread whipped cream filling on meringue shell to within 1 inch of the edge to create a border. Top with fruit in concentric circles (this looks beautiful with sliced strawberries) or pile the fruit on top for a less formal look.

Bars, Tarts, and Pies

When most people hear the word meringue, they can't help but think of pie. In fact, pie is where it all began for us. Meringue-topped pie, that is. Lemon Meringue, Black Bottom Pie, Key Lime Pie . . . . What would they be without mountains of soft, fluffy meringue and golden-tipped peaks?

While the previous chapter, Pavlovas, was all about hard meringue on the bottom, this chapter explores all the marvelous ways to use a soft meringue as a topping, not just for pies, but for tarts and bars, too.

Lemon Meringue Bars

Makes 24–36 bars, depending on size

Friends have been asking for Linda's lemon bars recipe for years. With a shortbread cookie crust and luscious lemon filling, they're so simple to make. We couldn't resist adding a meringue topping to create these dreamy bars.

CRUST
1 cup (2 sticks) unsalted butter, softened
1/2 cup powdered sugar
2 cups flour

LEMON FILLING
2 cups sugar
4 large eggs
1/3 cup flour
1 teaspoon baking powder
1/2 teaspoon salt
5 tablespoons fresh lemon juice
1 teaspoon lemon zest

MERINGUE TOPPING
4 large egg whites, room temperature
Tiny pinch of salt
1/2 cup superfine sugar

CRUST: Preheat oven to 350 degrees.

In the bowl of an electric stand mixer, beat butter and powdered sugar until creamy. Add flour and beat thoroughly. Press the mixture into a well-greased 9 x 13-inch baking pan. Bake for 20 minutes.

LEMON FILLING: Combine all the ingredients in a medium bowl and beat until smooth and well-combined. Pour into warm baked crust and bake for another 25 minutes.

MERINGUE TOPPING: In the bowl of an electric stand mixer fitted with the whisk attachment, beat egg whites on medium-high until foamy. Add salt and continue beating until soft peaks form. Add sugar, about a tablespoon at a time, and beat on high until peaks are stiff and glossy. Spread meringue over the lemon filling with a spatula or the back of the spoon, swirling to make pretty peaks. Return to oven and bake just until the meringue starts to turn golden brown, about 8–10 minutes. Let cool completely before cutting into bars. Refrigerate in an airtight container.

Golden Apricot Meringue Bars

Makes 9 bars

At their best, apricots are sweet, honey-like, and dense with flavor, making them the perfect canvas for sugary clouds of meringue. From the buttery shortbread crust to the caramelized brown sugar apricot filling, each layer of these luscious bars is pure gold.

SHORTBREAD CRUST
1/2 cup (1 stick) unsalted butter, softened
2 tablespoons firmly packed brown sugar
2 tablespoons sugar
1 cup flour
1/8 teaspoon kosher salt

APRICOT LAYER
1 cup (6 ounces) dried apricots
1 cup firmly packed brown sugar
1/3 cup flour

2 large eggs, lightly beaten
1/4 cup apricot jam
1/2 teaspoon baking powder
1/2 teaspoon pure vanilla extract
1/4 teaspoon salt

MERINGUE TOPPING
2 large egg whites, room temperature
Tiny pinch of salt
1/4 cup superfine sugar

SHORTBREAD CRUST: Preheat oven to 350 degrees.

In the bowl of an electric stand mixer, beat butter and both sugars until creamy. Add flour and salt, and beat thoroughly. Press the mixture into a well-greased 8 x 8 x 2-inch square baking pan. Bake for 20 minutes, until golden.

APRICOT LAYER: In a small saucepan, cover apricots with water and bring to a boil over high heat. Reduce heat to simmer, and cook until plumped, about 15 minutes. Drain well and finely chop. Transfer chopped apricots to the bowl of your electric mixer. Add remaining ingredients and beat on medium until combined, scraping down the bowl, if needed. Pour apricot mixture over crust, and bake until top is golden, about 22 minutes.

MERINGUE TOPPING: In the bowl of an electric mixer fitted with the whisk attachment, beat egg whites until foamy. Add salt and increase speed to medium-high; continue beating until soft peaks form. Add sugar, about a tablespoon at a time, and beat on high until meringue is glossy with stiff peaks. Spread this topping over the apricot filling with a spatula or the back of a spoon, swirling to make pretty peaks. Return pan to oven and bake just until the meringue starts to turn golden brown, about 8–10 minutes. Remove from oven and cool completely before cutting into bars. Cover and refrigerate any leftovers.

Toll House Halfway Bars

Makes 24–36 bars, depending on size

If you love Toll House cookies, you'll love these gooey, chocolaty meringue cookie bars—especially when warm from the oven. Recipes for halfway bars can be found in many of those old spiral-bound church and community recipe books. We've seen various explanations of why these bars are called "halfway." Could it be because they're so delicious, you feel as though you are halfway to heaven?

HALFWAY BARS
2 cups whole wheat flour*
1 teaspoon baking powder
1/2 teaspoon baking soda
1 teaspoon salt
1 cup (2 sticks) unsalted butter, softened
1 cup firmly packed light brown sugar
1/2 cup sugar
2 egg yolks (save whites for meringue topping)
1 tablespoon water
1 1/2 teaspoons pure vanilla extract
2 cups semisweet chocolate chips

BROWN SUGAR MERINGUE TOPPING
2 large egg whites, room temperature
Pinch of salt
1/2 cup firmly packed light brown sugar

HALFWAY BARS: Preheat oven to 350 degrees.

Line a 9 x 13-inch baking pan with parchment paper or foil, allowing it to hang over the pan edges—this will help you to remove the bars from the pan later. Spray paper or foil with nonstick cooking spray.

Combine flour, baking powder, baking soda, and salt in a medium bowl; set aside.

In an electric stand mixer, on medium speed, beat butter, brown sugar, and sugar until well blended. Add egg yolks, water, and vanilla and mix until well incorporated. Reduce speed to low and add flour mixture until just combined; mix in chocolate chips. Spread batter evenly in baking pan.

BROWN SUGAR MERINGUE TOPPING: In the bowl of an electric stand mixer fitted with the whisk attachment, beat egg whites until foamy. Add salt and continue beating on medium-high speed until soft peaks form. Reduce speed to medium and add brown sugar, about a tablespoon at a time, until all the sugar has been added. Stop mixer and scrape down sides of the bowl then resume beating on high until stiff, glossy peaks form.

Spread meringue over chocolate chip layer and bake until golden brown, about 35–40 minutes. Cool for about 15 minutes before lifting out of the pan using the parchment or foil overhang. Cut into bars and enjoy while they're still warm.

Note: Warm leftover bars for a few seconds in the microwave to get the chocolate gooey again.

*You can substitute white flour, but the whole wheat gives the bars a dense, slightly nutty flavor.

Mom's Sky-High Lemon Meringue Pie

Serves 8

Growing up, Linda would ask her mom to make lemon meringue pie for her birthday because it was her absolute favorite dessert. It still is today. The flaky, slightly salty crust, mouth watering lemon filling, and airy double height meringue topping is a wonderful combination of tastes and textures. Truth be told, on the rare occasion that there's any leftover, Linda actually prefers it the next day.

PIE CRUST
1 1/2 cups flour
1/2 teaspoon kosher salt
1/2 cup vegetable shortening
2 1/2 to 3 tablespoons ice water, divided

LEMON FILLING
1 1/2 cups sugar
1/3 cup cornstarch
1/4 teaspoon salt
1 1/2 cups water
4 egg yolks, slightly beaten (save the egg whites for the meringue)
2 to 2 1/2 tablespoons grated lemon zest (from about 4 medium lemons)
2 tablespoons unsalted butter
1/4 cup lemon juice (from about 2 medium lemons)

MERINGUE
8 large egg whites, room temperature
1/2 teaspoon cream of tartar
1/2 teaspoon salt
1 1/3 cups superfine sugar

PIE CRUST: In the bowl of your food processor, pulse flour and salt a few times just to combine. Add shortening and process until the mixture resembles coarse meal with some pea-size pieces. With the food processor running, slowly add water in a steady stream, 1 tablespoon at a time, until the dough holds together when you squeeze a bit in your hand. If it's too crumbly, add a little more water. Make sure you don't add too much water—you don't want the dough to be sticky. Flatten the ball into a disc and wrap in plastic wrap; refrigerate for 1 hour or more.

Lemon Meringue Pie (continued)

Remove pastry dough from the refrigerator and allow it to sit for about 5 minutes to soften slightly so it's easier to roll out. Place dough on the center of a lightly floured surface and sprinkle a little more flour over the surface of the dough. With a rolling pin, roll the dough from the center out to the edge, applying even pressure and rotating the rolling pin in various directions to create a circle, approximately 12 inches in diameter and of even thickness. Fold dough in half and carefully lift it into a 9-inch pie pan. Unfold and gently ease dough into the pan so that 1 inch of the pastry overhangs the edge all around; trim off any excess. Create a ruffled edge by pressing the knuckles of your first two fingers, spread about an inch apart, into the edge as you work your way around the entire crust. Refrigerate 1 hour or more before baking.

Preheat oven to 450 degrees.

Prick bottom and sides of pie shell with fork to vent steam and prevent shrinkage. Bake 12–15 minutes or until golden brown. Cool on wire rack.

LEMON FILLING: In heavy-bottom medium saucepan, combine sugar, cornstarch, and salt. Gradually stir in water. Bring to boil over medium heat, stirring constantly. Boil 1 minute; mixture will be thickened and translucent. Remove from heat. Add a little of the hot mixture into egg yolks in a small bowl, whisking constantly; pour tempered egg mixture back into saucepan and add the lemon zest. Stir constantly over medium heat until mixture boils again, about 1 minute. Remove from heat and add butter, stirring until melted. Gradually stir in lemon juice. Pour into center of pie crust. Let cool while making meringue.

MERINGUE: Preheat oven to 375 degrees.

In the bowl of an electric stand mixer fitted with the whisk attachment, beat egg whites and cream of tartar until foamy. Add salt and beat on medium-high until soft peaks form. Add sugar, about a tablespoon at a time, and continue beating on high until peaks are stiff and glossy.

TO ASSEMBLE PIE: With a teaspoon, place meringue in mounds all the way around the outer edge of the pie where the filling meets the crust to form a seal. This will prevent the meringue from pulling away from the crust when baking. Pile remaining meringue in center and spread it to cover the entire surface of the pie. Using the back of your spoon, form decorative swirls and peaks across the pie. Bake 12–15 minutes or until lightly browned. Remove from oven and cool on a wire rack. Make sure the bottom of pie is at room temperature before slicing. Store any leftover pie in the refrigerator.

Vanilla Meringue Pear Tart

Serves 6

Everyone loves the warm pear tart Jennifer brings to dinner parties in the winter months, though she confesses it's one of the simplest desserts to make. The white peach liqueur really brings out the flavor of the pears, and the vanilla meringue topping is heaven.

TART CRUST
1 cup flour
1/2 cup (1 stick) unsalted butter, cut into chunks
1 tablespoon plus 1 teaspoon sugar
Big pinch of salt
2 tablespoons ice water

PEAR FILLING
3 ripe Bartlett pears
4 tablespoons sugar
1 tablespoon white peach liqueur (such as Fassbind)
3 tablespoons unsalted butter, cut into tiny pieces

VANILLA MERINGUE TOPPING
2 large egg whites, room temperature
Pinch of cream of tartar
1/3 cup superfine sugar
1 teaspoon pure vanilla extract

TART CRUST: In the bowl of your food processor, combine flour, butter, sugar, and salt and pulse for 30 seconds, just until combined. With food processor running, drizzle water into the opening until the dough just forms into a ball. Scoop out ball of dough, wrap in plastic wrap, and chill for at least 1 hour.

Thinly roll out tart crust and line a 9-inch tart pan with the dough. Chill the dough while you prepare the pear filling.

PEAR FILLING: Preheat oven to 400 degrees.

Peel and core pears and cut them into quarters; then slice them as thinly as possible. Take the chilled tart crust out of the refrigerator and layer the pear slices all along the bottom of the crust, overlapping slices (they will shrink when baked). Sprinkle pears with sugar and liqueur and then dot the surface with pieces of butter. Bake for about 45 minutes, until the crust is golden and the pears are starting to caramelize.

Vanilla Meringue Pear Tart (continued)

Take tart out of oven to cool. Turn oven down to 375 degrees and make topping while the oven adjusts temperature.

VANILLA MERINGUE TOPPING: In the bowl of an electric stand mixer fitted with the whisk attachment, beat egg whites and cream of tartar on medium-high until soft peaks form. Add sugar, about a tablespoon at a time, and continue beating on high until meringue has stiff, glossy peaks. Add vanilla and beat for another 30 seconds until combined.

ASSEMBLE TART: With a spoon, spread meringue over the top of the pear tart, forming a seal at the edge so that the meringue does not shrink away from the crust during baking. Using the back of your spoon, form decorative swirls and peaks across the top of the tart. Bake for about 12 minutes or until golden on top. Remove from oven and cool for a few minutes on a wire rack before serving.

Key Lime Pie

Serves 8

One bite of this creamy, zesty pie topped with impossibly light meringue and you will be transported to the sunny Florida Keys. Please do not use regular limes. If you cannot find Key limes or Key lime juice in your local grocery store, you can find them online.

PIE CRUST
1 1/4 cups graham cracker crumbs
1/4 cup sugar
5 tablespoons unsalted butter, melted

KEY LIME FILLING
6 large egg yolks (save whites for meringue topping)

1 (14-ounce) can sweetened condensed milk
3/4 cup Key lime juice
Zest of 1 Key lime

MERINGUE TOPPING
6 large egg whites, room temperature
5 tablespoons superfine sugar

PIE CRUST: Preheat oven to 350 degrees.

In a medium bowl, combine graham cracker crumbs, sugar, and butter. Using your fingers or the bottom of a measuring cup, evenly press mixture into 9 1/2-inch pie or tart pan from the center to the outside of the pan. Bake for 6–8 minutes. Cool on a wire rack.

KEY LIME FILLING: In the bowl of an electric mixer fitted with a paddle attachment, beat yolks and condensed milk until blended; add lime juice and zest and beat until incorporated. Pour into pie crust.

MERINGUE TOPPING: Preheat oven to 300 degrees.

In the bowl of an electric stand mixer fitted with the whisk attachment, beat egg whites until soft peaks form. Gradually add the sugar, about a tablespoon at a time, beating on high, until meringue is stiff with glossy peaks.

With a teaspoon, mound meringue all the way around the outer edge of the pie where the filling meets the crust to form a seal. This will prevent the meringue from pulling away from the crust when baking. Spread the remaining meringue onto lime filling, making pretty peaks throughout the top with a spoon or spatula. Bake for 25–30 minutes, until meringue tips are golden. Remove from oven and cool on a wire rack. Make sure the bottom of pie is at room temperature before slicing. Store any leftover pie in the refrigerator.

Blood Orange Curd Meringue Tart with Dark Chocolate

Serves 8

This tart is based on a recipe Jennifer and her cooking students created for celebrity chef and radio host Evan Kleiman's "Good Food" Pie Contest a few years ago and it was a huge hit with both the kids and adults. The flavors of blood orange and dark chocolate are sublime.

CHOCOLATE COOKIE CRUST
1 1/2 cups chocolate cookie crumbs (from approximately 2 dozen chocolate wafer cookies)
1/3 cup sugar
Pinch of salt
1/4 cup (1/2 stick) unsalted butter, melted

BLOOD ORANGE CURD FILLING
1/2 cup blood orange juice (you can also use freshly squeezed clementine juice)
1 tablespoon lemon juice
6 large egg yolks (save 4 egg whites for meringue)
3 tablespoons cornstarch
2 tablespoons flour
3/4 cup sugar
1/2 cup (1 stick) unsalted butter,
    cut into 1/2-inch pieces, room temperature

MERINGUE TOPPING
4 large egg whites, room temperature
Pinch of cream of tartar
2 tablespoons superfine sugar

GARNISH
Dark chocolate curls
Zest of blood oranges, optional

CHOCOLATE COOKIE CRUST: Preheat oven to 375 degrees.

In a food processor, pulse cookies until the crumbs are fine. Add sugar, salt, and butter and pulse until combined. Press mixture into a 9 1/2-inch pie or tart pan, pushing up along the sides. Bake for 8 minutes, or until firm. Remove from oven to cool.

BLOOD ORANGE CURD FILLING: Combine orange juice, lemon juice, egg yolks, cornstarch, flour, and sugar in a medium saucepan. Cook over medium heat, whisking constantly, for 8–10 minutes until sugar has dissolved and mixture has thickened. Remove from heat and add the butter a little at a time, stirring to fully combine. Pour filling into cooled tart crust.

MERINGUE TOPPING: In the bowl of an electric stand mixer fitted with the whisk attachment, beat egg whites and cream of tartar on medium-high speed until soft peaks form. Slowly add sugar, about a tablespoon at a time, and continue beating on high until peaks are glossy and stiff.

TO ASSEMBLE PIE: Preheat oven to 375 degrees.

Spread meringue over the top of the blood orange curd filling, making sure that the entire top of the tart is covered, mounding meringue around edges to form a seal. Bake for 10 minutes, or until the meringue is a light golden brown.

Take tart out of oven, let cool for at least 10 minutes, or chill for one hour for a firmer consistency. Just before serving, shave curls of dark chocolate along with blood orange zest, if desired, over the top of the meringue.

Southern Black Bottom Pie

Serves 8

Growing up in Tulsa, Jennifer was obsessed with the velvety Black Bottom Pie served at Pennington's Drive-Inn, a classic haunt from the 1950s. The chocolate cookie crust filled with a decadent chocolate layer and finished with chocolate and cognac-infused meringue topping most definitely earns this pie its name.

CRUST
1 Chocolate Cookie Crust (page 103–104)

BLACK BOTTOM FILLING
1/3 cup sugar
1/3 cup unsweetened Dutch-process cocoa powder
2 tablespoons cornstarch
Pinch of salt
1 1/2 cups whole milk
3 ounces bittersweet chocolate, finely chopped
2 tablespoons unsalted butter, cut into small pieces
1/2 teaspoon pure vanilla extract

TOPPING
1 1/2 teaspoons unflavored gelatin
2 tablespoons cold water
1/4 cup superfine sugar
1 tablespoon cornstarch
1/8 teaspoon salt
1 cup whole milk
1 teaspoon pure vanilla extract
1 tablespoon cognac

1/2 cup superfine sugar
Water (about 3 tablespoons)
4 large egg whites, room temperature

BLACK BOTTOM FILLING: Sift together sugar, cocoa powder, cornstarch, and salt into a medium saucepan. Gradually whisk in milk. Cook over medium-high heat, stirring constantly, until bubbles begin to form. Turn heat to low, add chocolate, and stir until chocolate has melted and mixture is thick, about 2–3 minutes. Remove from heat; whisk in butter and vanilla until smooth. Spread chocolate mixture over pie crust. Refrigerate about 1 hour.

TOPPING: The topping is made in two stages; first is a gelatin-based mixture flavored with cognac, followed by a meringue which is folded in to make it light and fluffy.

First stage: sprinkle gelatin over water in a small bowl. Let stand until soft, about 3 minutes; set aside.

Whisk sugar, cornstarch, and salt in a medium saucepan. Gradually whisk in milk. Cook over medium-high heat, stirring constantly, until mixture is thick and boiling, about 4 minutes. Remove from heat; stir in gelatin mixture, and let cool completely. Stir in vanilla and cognac. Briefly place pan in an ice-water bath to thicken slightly, if needed. Do not let it set completely. Let cool a bit while you make meringue.

Second stage: bring sugar and water to a boil in a small saucepan, stirring to dissolve sugar. Brush down sides of pan with a wet pastry brush to prevent crystals from forming. Boil, without stirring, until syrup registers 235 degrees on a candy thermometer.

Meanwhile, in the bowl of an electric stand mixer fitted with the whisk attachment, beat egg whites until stiff peaks form. Gradually add hot sugar syrup and beat until all of the syrup has been incorporated and meringue becomes very glossy, approximately 6–8 minutes. Fold meringue mixture into gelatin mixture.

TO ASSEMBLE PIE: Spoon topping over Black Bottom Filling, covering it entirely. Refrigerate pie, uncovered, for about 2 1/2 hours, or overnight, before serving.

Caramelized Apple Tartlets

Makes 4

When not baking meringues, Linda loves to whip up the classic French dessert, Tarte Tatin. The apples in these beautiful little tarts are caramelized using a similar technique. Piled inside buttery pastry shells and topped with a feather-light meringue, we think our Caramelized Apple Tartlets are *très magnifique*.

SPECIAL EQUIPMENT: 4 (4-inch) nonstick fluted tart pans with removable bottoms.

PASTRY
1 cup flour
1 teaspoon sugar
1/4 teaspoon salt
1/3 cup cold unsalted butter, cut into pieces
2 to 2 1/2 tablespoons ice water

CARAMELIZED APPLE FILLING
1/3 cup unsalted butter
1 cup plus 2 teaspoons sugar
5 Granny Smith or Golden Delicious apples, each peeled, cored, and cut into 8 slices
2 teaspoons flour

MERINGUE
2 large egg whites, room temperature
Pinch of salt
1/3 cup superfine sugar

PASTRY: In the bowl of your food processor, pulse flour, sugar, and salt a few times, just to combine. Add butter, 1 piece at a time, and process until the mixture resembles coarse meal with some pea-size pieces. With the food processor running, slowly add water in a steady stream, 1 tablespoon at a time, until the dough holds together when you squeeze a bit in your hand. If it's too crumbly, add a little more water. Make sure you don't add too much water or the pastry will be sticky. Flatten the ball into a disc and wrap in plastic wrap. Refrigerate for 1 hour or more.

When you're ready to roll out your crust, let the dough sit out a few minutes to soften a bit so it's easier to work with. On a lightly floured surface, roll the dough out to approximately 1/8-inch thickness. With a sharp knife, cut 4 circles about 5 inches in diameter. You can use the bottom of one of the tart pans as a guide, adding 1/2 inch all around. Place 1 circle of dough inside each tart pan, gently pressing it into place along the bottom and up the sides.

Caramelized Apple Tartlets (continued)

CARAMELIZED APPLE FILLING: In a medium-size heavy skillet, preferably cast iron, over medium heat, melt the butter. Add 1 cup sugar and stir until it is completely melted and turns into a bubbly, thick caramel brown syrup. Be careful not to burn it. Add the apples and stir occasionally to coat the apples with the caramel syrup. Cook for 15 minutes, uncovered.

Preheat oven to 400 degrees.

In a small bowl, mix together the remaining sugar and the flour; sprinkle a thin layer over the bottom of each of the pastries (this will help keep them crisp). Fill the pastries with caramelized apples, dividing them evenly between the 4 tart shells. Bake for 20 minutes. About 10 minutes before they're finished baking, begin making meringue. Remove from oven after 20 minutes, leaving heat on, but lowering temperature to 375 degrees.

MERINGUE: In the bowl of an electric stand mixer fitted with the whisk attachment, beat egg whites until foamy. Add salt and increase speed to medium-high, beating until soft peaks form. Add sugar, about a tablespoon at a time, and continue beating on high until meringue has stiff, glossy peaks.

TO ASSEMBLE TARTLETS: With a teaspoon, place meringue in mounds all the way around the outer edge of each tartlet where the filling meets the crust. You want the meringue to form a seal at the edge so that the meringue doesn't pull away from the crust when baking. Divide the remaining meringue evenly among the tartlets, spreading it to cover the entire surface. Using the back of your spoon, form decorative swirls and peaks. Bake for 12–15 minutes or until lightly browned. Remove from oven and cool for a few minutes on a wire rack before serving. These tartlets are also delicious at room temperature, but we like them best when they're still warm.

Cakes, Tortes, Vacherins, and Dacquoises

Dacquoise. Marjolaine. Meringata. Even the names of these desserts are dreamy. Though the recipes in this chapter may have one or two extra steps, they are still completely accessible to the home baker. Here you will find meringue masterpieces such as the dacquoise, an opulent dessert cake made of layers of nut meringue and whipped cream or buttercream, which takes its name from Dax, a town in Southwestern France; and vacherin, a frozen dessert consisting of layers of meringue, whipped cream or ice cream, and sometimes fruit, and many more. As Johann Wolfgang von Goethe once said, "Whatever you can do, or dream you can, begin it. Boldness has genius, power, and magic in it." Meringue magic, of course.

Meyer Lemon Hazelnut Torte with Blackberry Sauce

Serves 8

Back in the late 1980s, we were regulars at City Restaurant in L.A., mostly because of Mary Sue Milliken and Susan Feniger's fabulous Lemon Hazelnut Tart, which was really more of a torte. Our crispy-crunchy ode to that dessert also has meringue in both the cake and the topping, and the hazelnuts are delicious with the sweeter Meyer lemons that we have substituted. We've also included a blackberry sauce, which takes it over the top.

CAKE
Baker's Joy or any nonstick flour-based baking spray
1 1/3 cups blanched almonds
1 1/3 cups blanched hazelnuts
1 1/2 tablespoons flour
3 large eggs, separated
3/4 cup sugar
Zest of 2 Meyer lemons (reserve the juice)
1 teaspoon pure vanilla extract
Pinch of salt

MERINGUE LAYER AND TOPPING
3 large egg whites, room temperature
1 cup superfine sugar
Reserved ground nuts
Reserved Meyer lemon juice

BLACKBERRY SAUCE
1 pint fresh blackberries, rinsed and dried
1 tablespoon sugar
2 tablespoons freshly squeezed orange or tangerine juice

CAKE: Preheat the oven to 350 degrees and arrange a rack in the middle. Prepare a 9 or 10-inch removable-bottom cake pan with baking spray then line with a round of parchment paper and spray again. Set aside.

Place the nuts on a baking sheet and toast them for about 10 minutes, until they begin to smell "nutty" and turn slightly golden. Do not let them burn.

Meyer Lemon Hazelnut Torte (continued)

Place toasted nuts in a food processor and process in short bursts until they are finely ground. Place 1 cup of the nuts into a bowl with the flour and combine. Reserve remaining nuts.

In the bowl of a stand mixer, beat egg yolks and sugar on medium speed until pale yellow. Add lemon zest and vanilla and beat again for another minute. Transfer to a bowl and set aside.

In a clean bowl of an electric stand mixer fitted with the whisk attachment, beat egg whites until foamy then add salt and beat on medium-high until soft peaks form.

Fold in the nut mixture, making sure not to deflate the beaten egg whites then gently fold into lemon mixture.

Pour into prepared cake pan and bake for about 25 minutes, until the cake is slightly golden on top and a toothpick inserted in the middle comes out clean.

Allow cake to cool a bit then remove from pan by running a knife along the inside of the pan and inverting onto a parchment paper-lined baking sheet. Continue to cool while making meringue topping.

MERINGUE LAYER AND TOPPING: Lower oven temperature to 300 degrees.

In a clean bowl of an electric stand mixer fitted with the whisk attachment, beat egg whites on medium-high until soft peaks form. Gradually add sugar, about a tablespoon at a time, beating on high until peaks are stiff. Fold in reserved ground nuts.

Spread meringue onto the cake then drizzle with Meyer lemon juice. Bake for about 40 minutes, until the meringue is crispy on top. Set aside to cool until ready to serve.

BLACKBERRY SAUCE: Place the ingredients into a blender, or use an immersion blender, and blend everything together until it becomes a blackberry purée. Strain into a bowl.

TO ASSEMBLE AND SERVE TORTE: When ready to serve, dust the top of the torte with powdered sugar, cut into slices, and serve with blackberry sauce.

Almond Marjolaine with Praline Buttercream

Serves 6

The beautiful, delicately layered French marjolaine is rectangular and consists of many layers of nut-meringue and buttercream filling. Our version includes both almonds and pecans. There are many steps in this recipe, but be patient. Every bite of this decadent masterpiece is worth it.

NUT MERINGUE LAYERS
Baker's Joy or any nonstick flour-based baking spray
1 cup blanched whole almonds
1/3 cup flour
2 tablespoons unsweetened cocoa powder
6 large egg whites, room temperature (save yolks for custard)
1 cup superfine sugar

PRALINE
1 cup sugar
2/3 cup blanched whole pecans

CUSTARD BUTTERCREAM
1/2 cup milk
1 cup sugar
1 teaspoon pure vanilla extract
6 large egg yolks
2 cups (4 sticks) unsalted butter, softened

TOPPING
1/2 cup pecans, toasted, cooled, and chopped
Powdered sugar

NUT MERINGUE LAYERS: Preheat oven to 350 degrees. Line a 10 x 15-inch jelly roll pan with parchment paper, leaving the paper longer than the sides so you can lift the baked meringue out of the pan. Spray with baking spray.

In a food processor, pulse almonds until fine; then add flour and cocoa and pulse again until mixture is very fine.

In the bowl of an electric stand mixer fitted with the whisk attachment, beat egg whites until soft peaks form, and then slowly add sugar, about a tablespoon at a time, and beat on high until you have stiff peaks.

Fold almond mixture into meringue, being careful not to deflate it. Pour the mixture into jelly roll pan, evenly smoothing it across the pan. Bake in middle of oven for 30–35 minutes, or until firm to the touch.

Carefully lift the edges of the parchment paper to remove meringue from pan and place on wire rack to cool. Once it is cool, gently peel parchment off of meringue.

PRALINE: Line a baking sheet with foil.

In a dry heavy-bottom small saucepan, cook sugar over moderate heat, stirring with a fork, until melted. Cook, without stirring, swirling the pan, until it turns to a golden caramel. Remove pan from heat and stir in pecans. Immediately pour mixture onto baking sheet, tilting the sheet to make a thin layer; cool completely.

Break praline into pieces and transfer to a sturdy ziplock bag, flattening the bag to remove the air before sealing it. Crush praline into coarse pieces with a rolling pin.

Note: Praline may be made up to a week in advance and kept in an airtight container at room temperature.

CUSTARD BUTTERCREAM: In a small saucepan, simmer milk, sugar, and vanilla; stir until sugar is dissolved.

In a medium bowl, whisk yolks and then slowly (you don't want to scramble the eggs) add warm milk mixture in a steady stream, whisking constantly. Transfer mixture to saucepan and cook over low heat, stirring, until a candy thermometer registers 170 degrees. Pour custard mixture through a strainer into a bowl and cool completely.

In the bowl of an electric stand mixer, beat butter until light and fluffy then beat in custard, a little at a time, until smooth. Beat in 1/2 cup praline, reserving remaining praline for garnish.

TO ASSEMBLE MARJOLAINE: Place meringue onto work surface and cut in half, then cut in half again so you have 4 rectangles. Spread buttercream on top of each layer then stack them evenly on top of one another. Use an offset spatula to cover the sides with the remaining buttercream.

Gently press topping pecans onto top and sides of marjolaine and dust with powdered sugar. Garnish with some of the leftover praline and serve.

Note: Marjolaine may be made 1 day ahead and chilled, covered. Let it stand at cool room temperature an hour or two before serving. Give it a final dusting of powdered sugar just before serving.

Coconut Meringue Cake with Lavender Flowers

Makes 1 double-layer 9-inch round cake (serves approximately 8)

Lavender is so delicate and beautiful, and when paired with vanilla, it is divine. Here we have brought together coconut and vanilla with fragrant fresh lavender flowers for the lightest, moistest meringue cake imaginable.

CAKE BATTER

Baker's Joy or any nonstick flour-based baking spray
3 1/2 cups cake flour
1 tablespoon plus 1 teaspoon baking powder
3/4 teaspoon salt
1 cup unsweetened coconut milk
2 teaspoons pure vanilla extract
1 cup (2 sticks) unsalted butter, softened
1 2/3 cups sugar

MERINGUE (TO BE FOLDED INTO CAKE BATTER)

8 large egg whites, room temperature
1/2 teaspoon cream of tartar
Pinch of salt
1/3 cup superfine sugar

BUTTERCREAM FROSTING

1 cup (2 sticks) unsalted butter, softened
1 bag (2 pounds or approximately 6 cups) powdered sugar
1 teaspoon pure vanilla extract
Pinch of salt
2 to 3 tablespoons unsweetened coconut milk

TOPPING AND GARNISH

1 to 2 cups sweetened shredded coconut
2 tablespoons lavender flowers, washed and dried
   (if not available, you can use 1/2 teaspoon dried culinary lavender)
1 sprig fresh lavender, washed and dried, optional

Coconut Meringue Cake (continued)

CAKE BATTER: Preheat oven to 350 degrees. Spray 2 (9-inch) round cake pans with baking spray.

Combine flour, baking powder, and salt in a medium bowl. In a small bowl, combine coconut milk and vanilla; set both aside.

In an electric stand mixer, beat butter and sugar until fluffy. Add flour mixture to butter mixture in 2 parts, alternating with coconut milk mixture. Beat on low until smooth, scraping down sides of bowl, as needed. Set mixture aside while you make meringue.

MERINGUE: In a clean bowl of an electric stand mixer fitted with the whisk attachment, beat egg whites and cream of tartar on medium-high until soft peaks form. Beat in salt, then slowly add sugar, about a tablespoon at a time, and beat on high until stiff peaks form.

Fold a fourth of the meringue into cake batter to lighten. Then fold batter into remaining meringue. Divide the batter equally between the cake pans. Bake for about 40 minutes, or until a toothpick inserted into the center of the cake comes out clean. Watch it carefully in the beginning to make sure the top is not browning too quickly; if so, turn heat down slightly. Let cake cool in pans on wire racks while you make the frosting.

BUTTERCREAM FROSTING: In the bowl of an electric stand mixer, beat butter until creamy. Gradually, on slow speed, add the sugar, beating until incorporated. Add vanilla, salt, and half the coconut milk. Beat on high until glossy, adding the rest of the coconut milk, as needed for a spreadable consistency.

TO ASSEMBLE CAKE: When the cake is cool, invert the first layer onto a cake plate. Spread some of the buttercream across the entire surface and sprinkle lightly with lavender flowers then place the second cake layer on top. Frost the top and sides of the cake. Sprinkle coconut over top of cake and gently press onto sides, if desired, then sprinkle remaining lavender flowers all over the cake. Place sprig of fresh lavender on top for decoration.

Dark Chocolate Raspberry Dacquoise

Serves 10

Dark chocolate and raspberries are one of those perfect flavor combinations, like peanut butter and chocolate or peaches and cream. In this classic French recipe, circles of hazelnut meringue are layered with a chocolate mousse and then finished with a raspberry whipped cream and fresh raspberries.

MERINGUE LAYERS
5 ounces whole hazelnuts (about 2/3 cup), toasted and skinned
1 1/4 cups superfine sugar, divided
6 large egg whites, room temperature
Pinch of salt
1 teaspoon pure vanilla extract

DARK CHOCOLATE MOUSSE
7 ounces high quality dark or bittersweet chocolate (such as Valhrona or Callebaut)
2 cups heavy whipping cream, divided

RASPBERRY WHIPPED CREAM
1 cup heavy whipping cream
2 tablespoons sugar
1/2 teaspoon pure vanilla extract
1 cup fresh raspberries, rinsed and dried

TOPPINGS
1 cup fresh raspberries, rinsed and dried
Powdered sugar

MERINGUE LAYERS: Preheat oven to 275 degrees. Line 2 baking sheets with parchment paper. Draw 3 (7-inch) circles onto them.

In a food processor, pulse hazelnuts and 3/4 cup sugar until fine. Set aside.

In the bowl of an electric stand mixer fitted with the whisk attachment, beat egg whites on medium-high until foamy, then add salt and beat until peaks are soft. Add remaining sugar, beating until stiff peaks form; add vanilla and beat for another few seconds until incorporated. Gently fold hazelnut mixture into meringue, taking care not to deflate batter. Spoon meringue into a pastry bag fitted with a $1/2$-inch round tip. Pipe meringue in spirals on the parchment paper, covering the circles so that you have 3 meringue discs. (You may skip the pastry bag and just spoon the meringue into the circles.) Bake 20 minutes then turn heat down to 250 degrees and bake for another 45 minutes to 1 hour, until firm and dry to the touch. Take out and let cool.

DARK CHOCOLATE MOUSSE: Place chocolate into a stainless steel bowl. In a small saucepan, heat $3/4$ cup whipping cream until simmering. Pour cream over chocolate and stir until it has a ganache-like texture. Let cool.

Whip remaining cream to stiff peaks with electric mixer and fold into chocolate ganache. Set aside.

RASPBERRY WHIPPED CREAM: With an electric mixer, whip cream, sugar, and vanilla until stiff. Add the raspberries and whip again until incorporated.

TO ASSEMBLE AND SERVE DACQUOISE: Gently place 1 meringue disc onto a cake plate. Spread a third of the chocolate mousse on top of meringue, followed by a third of the raspberry whipped cream. Top with another meringue disc and repeat mousse and whipped cream until all the layers are stacked atop one another. Refrigerate for at least 1 hour, or up to 1 day. When ready to serve, garnish with fresh raspberries and a dusting of powdered sugar.

Chocolate-Flecked Meringata with Warm Espresso Fudge Sauce

Serves 8–10

We love how the warmth of the espresso fudge sauce contrasts with the frozen chocolate-flecked whipped cream nestled between layers of crisp meringue in this beautiful meringata (Italian for "meringued").

MERINGUE
6 large egg whites, room temperature
1/2 teaspoon cream of tartar
1 1/2 cups superfine sugar
1/4 teaspoon pure vanilla extract

CHOCOLATE-FLECKED WHIPPED CREAM FILLING
2 cups heavy whipping cream
1/3 cup powdered sugar
1 teaspoon pure vanilla extract
1/2 cup finely chopped bittersweet chocolate

WARM ESPRESSO FUDGE SAUCE
1/3 cup heavy whipping cream
3 tablespoons light corn syrup
3 tablespoons firmly packed brown sugar
2 tablespoons unsweetened cocoa powder
1 tablespoon espresso powder
1/8 teaspoon kosher salt
1/2 cup finely chopped bittersweet chocolate, divided
1 teaspoon pure vanilla extract

MERINGUE: Preheat oven to 225 degrees.

Trace 1 (10-inch) circle on each of 2 pieces of parchment paper then turn the paper over and place each on a large baking sheet.

In the bowl of an electric stand mixer fitted with the whisk attachment, beat egg whites and cream of tartar on medium-high speed until soft peaks form. Increase speed to high and gradually add sugar, about a tablespoon at a time, beating until stiff, glossy peaks form. Add vanilla and beat until incorporated.

Transfer half of the meringue to a pastry bag fitted with a $^1/_2$-inch plain round tip and pipe a ring of meringue just inside the line of 1 of the circles. Continue piping in concentric circles until the circle is completely filled. Repeat for the second circle. Bake for 90 minutes, rotating the baking sheets half way through. Turn oven off and cool meringue discs in closed oven, up to 2 hours or until dry to the touch. Cool completely before removing from the parchment paper.

CHOCOLATE-FLECKED WHIPPED CREAM FILLING: With an electric mixer, whip the cream, powdered sugar, and vanilla until stiff. Gently fold in chocolate.

WARM ESPRESSO FUDGE SAUCE: Bring cream, syrup, brown sugar, cocoa powder, espresso powder, salt, and $^1/_4$ cup chocolate to a boil in a small heavy-bottom saucepan over medium heat, stirring until chocolate is melted. Reduce heat and cook at a slow boil, stirring occasionally, 5 minutes. Remove from heat. Add vanilla and remaining chocolate and stir until smooth. Let cool slightly. The sauce can be made ahead and stored in the refrigerator in a covered container until you're ready to serve the meringata. Reheat the sauce on the stovetop or microwave until warm.

TO ASSEMBLE AND SERVE MERINGATA: Gently place 1 of the meringue discs on a flat, sturdy serving plate. With an offset spatula, spread the chocolate-flecked cream over meringue, spreading it to the edge. Top with the second meringue disc, pressing it very lightly into place. Cover with plastic wrap and freeze until the cream is firm, about 4 hours.

Remove the meringata cake from the freezer about 10–15 minutes before you're ready to serve so that the cream softens a bit, making it easier to slice. Using a serrated knife, cut the cake into wedges and transfer to individual dessert plates. Generously spoon the Warm Espresso Fudge Sauce over each piece and serve. If you have any of the meringata leftover, return it to the freezer, covered in plastic wrap or foil.

Peaches and Cream Ginger-Meringue Shortcakes

Makes 4

Our take on this classic American dessert replaces the traditional biscuit shortcakes with what else—a meringue—with just a hint of ginger. The whipped cream is sweetened with brown sugar to round out the flavor in this sophisticated dessert that's so perfect in the summertime when peaches are sweet and plentiful.

GINGER-MERINGUE SHORTCAKES
$1/2$ cup superfine sugar
$1 1/2$ teaspoons cornstarch
2 large egg whites, room temperature
$1/8$ teaspoon cream of tartar
$1/4$ teaspoon ground ginger

PEACHES
3 cups peaches (from 3 to 4 fresh peaches)

3 tablespoons sugar (more or less, depending on how sweet the peaches are)

BROWN SUGAR WHIPPED CREAM
$3/4$ cup heavy whipping cream
2 tablespoons firmly packed brown sugar
$1/2$ teaspoon pure vanilla extract

GINGER-MERINGUE SHORTCAKES: Preheat oven to 275 degrees. In a small bowl, whisk together sugar and cornstarch; set aside.

In the bowl of an electric stand mixer fitted with the whisk attachment, beat egg whites and cream of tartar on medium-high speed until soft peaks form. Decrease speed to medium and gradually add sugar mixture, about a tablespoon at a time. When all the sugar mixture is incorporated, increase speed to high and beat until stiff, glossy peaks have formed. Add ginger and beat just until incorporated.

On baking sheets lined with parchment paper, use a spoon to form 8 meringue shortcakes, approximately 3 inches in diameter. Bake for 30 minutes. Turn off heat and leave in the oven for 1 hour to continue drying. Remove from oven to cool. If not using right away, store in an airtight container.

PEACHES: If you prefer peaches without skin, blanch peaches to loosen their skin by submerging them in a pot of boiling water for 1 minute. Immediately remove from boiling water and place in a bowl of ice water. Remove the skin with your fingers then slice or dice peaches. Transfer to a medium-size bowl and gently toss with sugar. Cover and refrigerate for 1 hour or more.

BROWN SUGAR WHIPPED CREAM: With an electric mixer, whip the cream, sugar, and vanilla until firm.

TO ASSEMBLE SHORTCAKES: Place 1 meringue shortcake on each of 4 individual dessert plates. On top of each meringue, add a dollop of whipped cream, a fourth of the peaches, followed by another dollop of whipped cream. Top with another meringue shortcake.

Raspberry White Chocolate Vacherin

Serves 8–10

A vacherin—named for its resemblance to a wheel of cow's milk cheese made in France and Switzerland—is sort of a frozen meringue torte. When Linda created this gorgeous vacherin to take to a party, everyone swooned over its exquisite layers of crisp, yet slightly chewy pink meringue, white chocolate whipped cream, and bright raspberries.

MERINGUE
6 large egg whites, room temperature
1/2 teaspoon cream of tartar
1 1/2 cups superfine sugar
2 1/2 teaspoons raspberry extract

FILLING
2 cups heavy whipping cream
4 tablespoons powdered sugar
1 teaspoon pure vanilla extract
1/2 cup finely chopped white chocolate
1 1/2 cups fresh raspberries rinsed and dried or 12 ounces frozen, thawed, and drained

MERINGUE: Preheat oven to 225 degrees.

Trace 1 (10-inch) circle on each of 2 pieces of parchment paper then turn the paper over and place each on a large baking sheet.

In the bowl of an electric stand mixer fitted with the whisk attachment, beat egg whites and cream of tartar on medium-high speed until soft peaks form. Gradually add sugar, about a tablespoon at a time, beating on high until meringue has stiff, glossy peaks. Add raspberry extract and beat just until incorporated.

Transfer a little over half of the meringue to a pastry bag fitted with a 1/2-inch star tip. Pipe a ring of stars just inside the line of each of the circles so that both the top and bottom meringues will have a decorative edge. To create the top meringue, continue piping concentric circles of stars very closely together, filling the entire surface of the ring. Fill in any gaps between the stars with more meringue. For the bottom meringue, you can follow the same steps as you did for the top meringue, or simply use the back of a spoon to evenly spread the remaining meringue inside the circle of stars, making sure that it fills the entire surface. (Since the bottom meringue will be covered with whipped cream and raspberries when the vacherin is assembled, no one will notice if the surface of this meringue disc isn't as decorative as the top layer.)

Bake for 90 minutes, rotating the baking sheets half way through. Turn oven off and cool meringue discs in closed oven, up to 2 hours or until dry to the touch. Cool completely before removing from the parchment paper.

FILLING: With an electric mixer, whip cream, powdered sugar, and vanilla until stiff. Fold in white chocolate.

TO ASSEMBLE AND SERVE VACHERIN: Carefully place the bottom meringue disc onto a flat serving plate. With a rubber spatula, evenly cover the surface with half of the whipped cream, making sure that it doesn't cover up the decorative star edge. Add the raspberries in an even layer then top with a layer of the remaining whipped cream. Gently place the second decorative meringue disc on top, pressing it ever so lightly into place. Carefully cover with plastic wrap and freeze until firm, about 4 hours.

Remove from the freezer about 10–15 minutes before you're ready to serve so that the cream and berries soften a bit, making it easier to slice. Using a serrated knife, cut the vacherin into wedges and transfer to individual dessert plates.

Moroccan Gateau Russe

Serves 6–8

Morocco has always held a certain mystique for Jennifer, and a recent trip there validated her hunch that their native cuisine is among the best in the world. One of Jennifer's Moroccan friends tells her that this gateau is actually French, but because Morocco was French-occupied for so many years, they embraced it as their own.

MERINGUE

Baker's Joy or any nonstick flour-based baking spray
6 large egg whites, room temperature
1/4 teaspoon cream of tartar
1/4 teaspoon salt
1 1/4 cups superfine sugar

CHOCOLATE FILLING AND TOPPINGS

1 cup hazelnuts, toasted and peeled, divided
  (reserving half —the prettiest ones—for garnish)
3 tablespoons superfine sugar, divided
8 ounces high-quality semisweet chocolate,
  broken into pieces
1/4 cup brewed coffee, optional
1 teaspoon Frangelica hazelnut liqueur
3 cups heavy whipping cream
Dark chocolate shavings

MERINGUE: Preheat the oven to 300 degrees.

Spray 3 (8-inch) removable-bottom cake pans with baking spray. Cut 3 rounds of parchment paper to line the bottom of each pan and generously spray again. Make sure the sides of the pan are sprayed as well for easy removal of meringue.

In the bowl of an electric stand mixer fitted with the whisk attachment, beat egg whites and cream of tartar until soft peaks form, then add salt. Slowly add sugar, about a tablespoon at a time, and continue beating on high until stiff peaks form.

Divide the meringue between the 3 pans and smooth the tops with a spatula. Place in the oven and immediately lower temperature to 275 degrees. Bake until the meringue is firm, about 1 hour. Turn off oven and let meringues stand for a few hours or overnight to continue to crisp.

When you are ready to assemble the gateau, remove meringues from pans and carefully peel the paper from the bottom of each disc.

Note: If the meringues stick, they are not dry enough. You can put them back into the oven at 200 degrees for 5–10 more minutes then let completely cool.

CHOCOLATE FILLING AND TOPPINGS: In a food processor, grind $1/2$ cup of nuts with 1 tablespoon sugar until you have a fine meal. Combine the chocolate, coffee, Frangelica, and remaining sugar in a heatproof bowl and place over a pot of simmering water, or use a double boiler. Stir until chocolate melts. Set aside to cool.

In a large bowl, whip cream with an electric mixer on high until stiff. Gently fold the melted chocolate into the whipped cream and then fold in the ground nuts.

TO ASSEMBLE GATEAU: Place 1 meringue disc on a serving platter. With a spatula, spread a third of the chocolate filling over the top. Cover with a second disc and repeat. Top the third disc with the remaining chocolate filling, spreading it all around the sides and top of the cake. Garnish with remaining whole hazelnuts and shaved chocolate. Refrigerate for 2–3 hours before serving.

Clementine Meringue Cake with Rosemary

Makes 1 double-layer 9-inch round cake (serves approximately 8)

The scent of clementine with rosemary reminds us of being in Tuscany, but that's not where this meringue-lightened cake was inspired. It was actually The Hungry Cat restaurant in Hollywood, where Jennifer enjoyed a cocktail infused with these flavors. It wasn't a huge leap to assume it would be delicious in this heavenly meringue cake creation.

CAKE

Baker's Joy or any nonstick flour-based baking spray
$3\frac{1}{2}$ cups cake flour
1 tablespoon plus 1 teaspoon baking powder
$\frac{1}{2}$ teaspoon salt
1 cup (2 sticks) unsalted butter, softened
$1\frac{2}{3}$ cups sugar
1 tablespoon clementine zest
$\frac{1}{2}$ teaspoon pure vanilla extract
$1\frac{1}{2}$ tablespoons clementine juice
1 cup milk

MERINGUE (TO BE FOLDED INTO CAKE BATTER)

8 large egg whites, room temperature
Pinch of cream of tartar
Pinch of salt
$\frac{1}{3}$ cup superfine sugar

CLEMENTINE ROSEMARY BUTTERCREAM FROSTING

1 cup (2 sticks) unsalted butter, softened
1 bag (2 pounds or approximately 6 cups) powdered sugar
$\frac{1}{2}$ teaspoon pure vanilla extract
Pinch of salt
2 tablespoons clementine juice
1 teaspoon clementine zest
1 teaspoon fresh rosemary, very finely chopped, divided

GARNISH

1 clementine, sliced
1 sprig rosemary, optional

CAKE: Preheat the oven to 350 degrees and arrange a rack in the middle. Prepare 2 (9-inch) round cake pans; spray with baking spray then line each with a round of parchment paper and spray again. Set aside.

Combine flour, baking powder, and salt in a medium bowl; set aside. In large bowl, with an electric mixer, beat butter and sugar until light and fluffy. Add zest, vanilla, and juice and beat again until incorporated.

Add flour mixture to butter mixture in 2 parts, alternating with milk. Beat on low until smooth, scraping down the sides of the bowl.

Clementine Meringue Cake (continued)

MERINGUE: In a clean bowl of an electric stand mixer fitted with the whisk attachment, beat egg whites and cream of tartar on medium-high until soft peaks form. Add salt, then slowly add sugar, about a tablespoon at a time, and beat on high until peaks are stiff.

Fold in a fourth of the meringue into cake batter to lighten. Then fold batter into remaining meringue.

Pour into prepared cake pans. Bake for 40 minutes, or until a toothpick inserted into the center comes out clean. Let cake cool while you make the frosting.

CLEMENTINE ROSEMARY BUTTERCREAM FROSTING: In an electric stand mixer, beat butter until creamy. Gradually, and on slow speed, add the sugar, beating until incorporated. Add vanilla, salt, juice, zest, and $1/2$ teaspoon rosemary. Beat on high until glossy, adding more juice, if necessary, for a spreadable consistency.

TO ASSEMBLE CAKE: When cake is cool, invert the first layer onto a cake plate. Spread some of the buttercream onto the first cake layer then place the second cake layer on top. Frost the entire cake.

Sprinkle remaining rosemary lightly over frosting. Garnish with slices of clementine right in the middle of the cake and place sprig of rosemary into it, if using.

Vacherin with Lemon Curd and Strawberries

Serves 6

The first time Jennifer tasted this gorgeous confection at a tea salon in Paris, it was layered with lemon curd and topped with strawberries, and while there are many versions, this is still her favorite. It sounds elaborate, but once you have the hang of making meringue, it's actually just a matter of assembling it.

MERINGUES
6 large egg whites, room temperature (reserve egg yolks for the curd)
1/4 teaspoon cream of tartar
Pinch of salt
1 cup superfine sugar
1/2 teaspoon pure vanilla extract

LEMON CURD
6 egg yolks
1 cup superfine sugar
Zest and juice of 4 lemons
1/2 cup (1 stick) butter, cut into pieces

TOPPING
1 pint fresh strawberries, sliced
1 teaspoon sugar, optional

MERINGUES: Preheat oven to 250 degrees.

Trace 2 (8-inch) circles onto one sheet of parchment paper and 1 (8-inch) circle onto a second sheet of parchment. Place papers, marked side down, on baking sheets.

In the bowl of an electric stand mixer fitted with the whisk attachment, beat egg whites and cream of tartar on medium-high speed until soft peaks form; add salt. Beat in sugar, adding about a tablespoon at a time, until you have stiff, glossy peaks. Beat in vanilla.

Working in batches, spoon meringue into a large pastry bag fitted with a $1/2$-inch tip. Starting in center of each traced circle and holding tip just above paper, pipe meringue in spirals to fill circles, forming 3 disc shapes. If you don't have a pastry bag, simply spoon the meringue onto the parchment and spread into circles.

Bake meringues until firm, dry, and pale golden, about 2 hours. Turn off oven; leave meringues in oven with door closed at least 4 hours or overnight.

LEMON CURD: In a double boiler, or a metal bowl over simmering water, combine egg yolks and sugar and whisk until smooth, about 1 minute. Add zest and juice to egg mixture and whisk until smooth and thickened, approximately 8 minutes. You may have to remove the bowl from the heat from time to time to make sure the yolks don't curdle. When mixture is pale yellow and coats the back of a spoon, remove promptly from heat and stir in butter, 1 piece at a time, allowing each to melt before adding the next. Place curd into a bowl or plastic container and cover, laying a piece of plastic wrap directly on the surface of the curd. It can be stored in an airtight container for up to 2 weeks in the refrigerator.

TO ASSEMBLE AND SERVE VACHERIN: Gently place 1 of the meringue discs on a flat, sturdy serving plate. Spread a third of the lemon curd over the meringue, top with second meringue disc and then another third of the lemon curd. Top with remaining meringue disc and lemon curd. Cover with foil and freeze until firm, about 6 hours or up to 4 days.

About 10 minutes before you're ready to serve, remove vacherin from freezer to soften a bit. Top with strawberries sprinkled with sugar.

Meringue Frostings

Homemade frosting is so simple to make; we shudder at the thought of those little tubs of store-bought frosting. Even a simple cake-mix cake can be transformed with the real thing, which just takes a few minutes, or in the case of Seven-Minute Frosting, 7 minutes, to whip up. In contrast to a basic buttercream made with powdered sugar and butter, a meringue-based frosting is lighter, fluffier, and undeniably glossier. Once you taste our Salted Caramel Swiss Meringue Buttercream or Mocha Italian Meringue Buttercream frostings, you may find yourselves as hooked as we are.

Note: Contrary to popular belief, frosting and icing are not the same thing. Icing refers to a thin, glossy glaze such as that found on top of holiday cookies, whereas frosting is much thicker and fluffier, and is usually found on cakes.

Seven-Minute Frosting

Makes about 4 1/2 cups—enough to frost 1 triple-layer 9-inch round cake or 24 cupcakes

We love buttercream frosting, and the sweeter, the better, as far as we're concerned. However, one taste of this fluffy white meringue frosting, also known as marshmallow frosting, and it's easy to see why some people can't bear to frost their cakes and cupcakes with anything else.

3 large egg whites, room temperature
1 3/4 cups sugar
1/3 cup water
1/2 teaspoon cream of tartar
Pinch of salt
1 teaspoon pure vanilla extract

In a stainless steel bowl, whisk together egg whites, sugar, water, cream of tartar, and salt. Place the bowl over a pot of simmering water and immediately begin beating with an electric hand mixer on low speed. Beat for 1 minute and then increase the speed to high and continue to beat for 5 minutes. Remove from the heat and beat in the vanilla for 1 minute. Allow the frosting to cool for about 5 minutes before using. It can be made ahead of time and kept covered in the fridge until you are ready to use it.

Lemon Meringue Frosting

Makes about 3 cups—enough to frost 1 double-layer 9-inch round cake or 12 cupcakes

Not too sweet. Not too tart. This light, fluffy lemon meringue frosting is just right. It's the perfect complement to a vanilla or berry-flavored cake.

3 large egg whites, room temperature
1 cup sugar
3 tablespoons water
1/4 teaspoon cream of tartar
Pinch of salt
1 tablespoon finely grated lemon zest
2 teaspoons lemon juice
A drop or two of yellow food coloring, optional

In a stainless steel bowl, whisk together egg whites, sugar, water, and cream of tartar. Place the bowl over a pot of simmering water and immediately begin beating with an electric hand mixer on low speed. Beat for 1 minute and then increase the speed to high and continue to beat for 5 minutes. Turn off beater and add salt, lemon zest, and lemon juice, as well as food coloring, if using. Continue beating on high until stiff peaks form. You may need to scrape down the sides of the bowl and the beater blades to make sure that all the lemon zest is incorporated. Remove from heat and allow the frosting to cool before using.

Vanilla Swiss Meringue Buttercream

Makes about 4 cups —enough to frost 1 triple-layer 9-inch round cake or 24 cupcakes

Sometimes it's the simple things that really do taste the best, or at least it seems that way in the case of this light, silky smooth, buttery vanilla frosting. A classic.

4 large egg whites, room temperature
1 1/4 cups sugar
Pinch of salt
1 1/2 cups (3 sticks) unsalted butter, softened, divided
1 1/2 teaspoons pure vanilla extract
Food coloring, optional

In the bowl of an electric stand mixer, combine egg whites, sugar, and salt. Set bowl over a medium saucepan of simmering water and heat, whisking continually until sugar is dissolved, the mixture is white and frothy, and reaches 160 degrees on a candy thermometer.

Remove the bowl from the heat and attach it to your mixer. With the whisk attachment, beat on high speed until stiff peaks form and the mixture has cooled to room temperature, about 8 minutes. Reduce the speed to medium and add the butter, 1 tablespoon at a time, adding more once each addition of butter has been incorporated. Increase speed to medium-high and keep beating until the buttercream is thick and smooth, about 3–5 minutes. Don't worry if it looks lumpy or curdled during this process—it will eventually become smooth. Add vanilla and food coloring, if using, and beat just until blended.

Keep the buttercream at room temperature if you're using it right away. If you're piping it, you may want to let it firm up in the refrigerator for a few minutes first. You can also make it ahead of time and store it in the refrigerator for up to 3 days or in the freezer for up to 1 month. Just let it sit on your countertop until it reaches room temperature and beat it on low in your electric mixer to return the buttercream to a smooth consistency.

Salted Caramel Swiss Meringue Buttercream

Makes about 4 cups—enough to frost 1 triple-layer 9-inch round cake or 24 cupcakes

Heavily salted caramels are a traditional treat in the Brittany region of France. The sweet caramel in contrast to the local sea salt is simply divine. This frosting is so easy to make—the hardest part is not eating all the Salted Caramel Sauce before it's time to add it to the meringue buttercream.

SALTED CARAMEL SAUCE
1 cup sugar
¼ cup water
½ cup heavy whipping cream
A rounded ¼ teaspoon sea salt

SWISS MERINGUE BUTTERCREAM
4 large egg whites, room temperature
1 cup superfine sugar
¼ teaspoon cream of tartar
1½ cups (3 sticks) unsalted butter, softened, divided

SALTED CARAMEL SAUCE: Combine sugar and water in a small saucepan. Over low heat, cook the mixture, swirling the pan occasionally—don't stir—until the sugar dissolves. Increase to medium heat and continue cooking and swirling. Brush down sides of pan with a wet pastry brush to prevent crystals from forming.

While the sugar continues to bubble in the saucepan, microwave the cream on high for 1 minute; set aside.

Continue swirling the sugar in the saucepan until it reaches an amber color. Make sure it doesn't get too dark because it can quickly acquire a burnt taste. Remove from heat, and slowly and carefully (because it will steam and may splatter) pour the warmed cream into the saucepan, whisking the entire time so that the caramel doesn't harden into clumps. Stir in the sea salt and set aside to cool.

Note: The salted caramel sauce can be made up to a week in advance and stored in an airtight container in the refrigerator. Just bring it to room temperature before adding to the buttercream.

SWISS MERINGUE BUTTERCREAM: In the bowl of an electric stand mixer, combine egg whites and sugar. Set bowl over a medium saucepan of simmering water and heat, whisking continually until sugar is dissolved, the mixture is white and frothy, and reaches 160 degrees on a candy thermometer.

Remove the bowl from the heat and attach it to your mixer fitted with the whisk attachment. Add cream of tartar and beat on high until stiff peaks form and the mixture has cooled to room temperature, about 8 minutes. Reduce the speed to medium and add the butter, 1 tablespoon at a time, adding more once each addition of butter has been incorporated. Increase speed to medium-high and keep beating until the buttercream is thick and smooth, about 3–5 minutes.

Slowly pour 1 3/4 cups of the Salted Caramel Sauce into the buttercream and beat until incorporated and no streaks of the caramel remain.

You can keep the buttercream at room temperature if you're using it that day. If piping the frosting in a pastry bag, you may want to refrigerate for 10–15 minutes to allow it to firm up a bit. Drizzle remaining Salted Caramel Sauce over frosted cake or cupcakes.

Chocolate Swiss Meringue Buttercream

Makes about 4 cups—enough to frost 1 triple-layer 9-inch round cake or 24 cupcakes

This lovely chocolate frosting has an airy texture and a rich, buttery taste. Pipe it with a decorative tip to turn even the simplest of cupcakes into an exquisite dessert.

4 large egg whites, room temperature
1 1/4 cups sugar
1/4 teaspoon cream of tartar
1 1/2 cups (3 sticks) unsalted butter, softened, divided
1/2 teaspoon pure vanilla extract
1 cup semisweet chocolate morsels, melted

In the bowl of an electric stand mixer, combine egg whites and sugar. Set bowl over a medium saucepan of simmering water and heat, whisking continually until sugar is dissolved, the mixture is white and frothy, and reaches 160 degrees on a candy thermometer.

Remove the bowl from the heat and attach it to your mixer fitted with the whisk attachment. Add cream of tartar and beat on high speed until stiff peaks form and the mixture has cooled to room temperature, about 8 minutes. Reduce the speed to medium and add the butter, 1 tablespoon at a time, adding more once each addition of butter has been incorporated. Add vanilla and chocolate and beat on medium-high until the buttercream is thick and smooth, about 3–5 minutes.

Coconut Meringue Frosting

Makes about 3 cups—enough to frost 1 double-layer 9-inch round cake or 12 cupcakes

This sweet meringue frosting is flavored with coconut, which is particularly delicious on a rich chocolate cake. Once you've frosted your cake with this light, fluffy frosting, take it up a notch by sprinkling sweetened shredded coconut all over the top.

3 large egg whites, room temperature
1 3/4 cups sugar
1/3 cup water
1/2 teaspoon cream of tartar
Pinch of salt
1/2 teaspoon pure vanilla extract
1 teaspoon coconut extract
Sweetened shredded coconut, optional

In a stainless steel bowl, whisk together egg whites, sugar, water, cream of tartar, and salt. Place the bowl over a pot of simmering water and immediately begin beating with an electric hand mixer on low speed. Beat for 1 minute and then increase the speed to high and continue beating for 5 minutes. Remove from the heat and beat in vanilla and coconut extracts for 1 minute. Allow the frosting to cool for about 5 minutes before using. Sprinkle coconut on top and sides of cake, if desired.

Mocha Italian Meringue Buttercream

Makes about 4 cups—enough to frost 1 triple-layer 9-inch round cake or 24 cupcakes

Sometimes it takes a bit of trial and error to get something just right. We think we found the perfect balance of cocoa and espresso in this sophisticated mocha Italian meringue buttercream.

1 cup plus 2 tablespoons superfine sugar, divided
$1/4$ cup water
4 large egg whites, room temperature
$1/4$ teaspoon cream of tartar
$1 1/2$ cups (3 sticks) unsalted butter, softened, divided
1 tablespoon unsweetened cocoa powder
$2 1/2$ teaspoons ground espresso

Create sugar syrup by placing 1 cup sugar in a small saucepan then cover with water. Heat on medium, tilting and swirling the pan occasionally, but do not stir. Brush down sides of pan with a wet pastry brush to prevent crystals from forming. When all the sugar has dissolved, increase heat to medium-high and boil until the sugar syrup reaches 235 degrees, soft ball stage, on a candy thermometer. Immediately remove from heat.

Beat egg whites on medium-high in the bowl of an electric stand mixer fitted with the whisk attachment. When they are foamy, add cream of tartar and continue beating until soft peaks form. Add remaining sugar and beat. With the mixer running on medium speed, slowly pour the hot sugar syrup directly into the egg whites. Avoid pouring it onto the sides of the bowl or into the whisk. Increase speed to high and beat until stiff, glossy peaks form and the meringue has reached room temperature, about 5 minutes.

Reduce speed to medium and add butter, 1 tablespoon at a time, making sure the butter is incorporated between each addition. Add cocoa powder and espresso and beat just until incorporated. If piping the frosting in a pastry bag, you may want to refrigerate it for 10–15 minutes to allow it to firm up a bit.

Fresh Strawberry Italian Meringue Buttercream

Makes about 4 1/2 cups—enough to frost 1 triple-layer 9-inch round cake or 24 cupcakes

Fresh, ripe strawberries—so naturally juicy, fragrant, and abundant in summertime. Their natural sweetness combined with the silky meringue buttercream will transport you to summertime with just one taste, regardless of the season.

1 cup plus 2 tablespoons sugar, divided
1/4 cup water
4 large egg whites, room temperature
1/4 teaspoon cream of tartar
1 1/2 cups (3 sticks) unsalted butter, softened, divided
1/4 teaspoon pure vanilla extract
1/2 cup puréed fresh strawberries (from about 1 cup hulled strawberries)

Create sugar syrup by placing 1 cup sugar in a small saucepan then cover with water. Heat on medium, tilting and swirling the pan occasionally, but do not stir. Brush down sides of pan with a wet pastry brush to prevent crystals from forming. When all the sugar has dissolved, increase heat to medium-high and boil until the sugar syrup reaches 235 degrees, soft ball stage, on a candy thermometer. Immediately remove from heat.

Beat egg whites on medium-high in the bowl of an electric stand mixer fitted with the whisk attachment. When they are foamy, add cream of tartar and continue beating until soft peaks form. Add remaining sugar and beat. With the mixer running on medium speed, slowly pour the hot sugar syrup directly into the egg whites. Avoid pouring it onto the sides of the bowl or into the whisk. Increase speed to high and beat until stiff, glossy peaks form and the meringue has reached room temperature, about 5 minutes.

Reduce speed to medium and add butter, 1 tablespoon at a time, making sure the butter is incorporated between each addition. Add vanilla and strawberry purée and beat just until incorporated. If piping the frosting in a pastry bag, you may want to refrigerate it for 10–15 minutes to allow it to firm up a bit.

Heavenly Creations

"Light as a cloud," "ethereal," "heavenly." These are just some of the words to describe the sweet gossamer magic of meringue, and though it can be whipped up in minutes, why stop at traditional cookies, frostings, and desserts? In this chapter, we have taken simple meringue to its celestial limits and transformed it into some unforgettable—and truly heavenly—creations.

Meringue Ice Cream

Makes about 1 quart or 8 (^{1}/$_2$-cup) servings

On Linda's grand tour of Europe after graduate school, she made a pilgrimage to the world famous Vivoli gelateria in Florence, Italy, where she discovered their meringue gelato. She's not in the least bit embarrassed to admit that she went back an hour later for more! The taste of this meringue ice cream comes pretty close to the Vivoli version she remembers.

MERINGUES
2 large egg whites, room temperature
Pinch of cream of tartar
^{1}/$_2$ cup superfine sugar
^{1}/$_2$ teaspoon pure vanilla extract

ICE CREAM BASE
2 cups heavy cream
^{3}/$_4$ cup sugar
1 teaspoon pure vanilla extract
1 cup whole milk

MERINGUES: Preheat oven to 200 degrees.

In the bowl of an electric stand mixer fitted with the whisk attachment, beat egg whites and cream of tartar until foamy. Increase to medium-high and beat until soft peaks form. Gradually add sugar, about a tablespoon at a time, beating on high until stiff with glossy peaks. Beat in vanilla.

Drop by well-rounded teaspoons onto baking sheets lined with parchment paper, about 1 inch apart. Bake for 90 minutes. Turn off heat and leave meringues in the oven for 1 hour or more to crisp. Cool completely before removing from baking sheets. These cookies can be made a few days ahead and stored in an airtight container.

ICE CREAM BASE: Over medium heat in a heavy-bottom saucepan, heat the cream until small bubbles appear around the edge. Remove from heat and add the sugar, whisking until dissolved. Let the cream cool slightly. Add the vanilla to the whole milk then add to the cream mixture and whisk until combined. Cover and refrigerate until cold, or overnight.

Remove ice cream base from refrigerator and stir in broken pieces from 7 meringue cookies. Transfer immediately to the bowl of your ice cream maker, mixing and freezing according to manufacturer's directions. When the ice cream is very thick and almost done, break the remaining meringue cookies into large pieces and gently mix into the frozen ice cream. Serve immediately, or store in an airtight container in your freezer with a piece of plastic wrap covering the surface of the ice cream so that ice crystals do not form.

Baked Alaska

Serves 6

It took a few tries before Jennifer mastered this classic dessert, but by the time she did, her young cooking students were hooked on the sheer drama of this time-sensitive dessert, as well as the sensational combination of a frosty ice cream bombe and cake topped with warm, caramelized meringue. The recipe calls for two different flavors of ice cream, so feel free to experiment with your favorite combinations.

CHOCOLATE CAKE
Baker's Joy or any nonstick flour-based baking spray
1 cup boiling water
1/2 cup unsweetened cocoa powder
1 1/2 cups flour
1 teaspoon baking soda
1/4 teaspoon baking powder
1/2 teaspoon salt
1/2 cup (1 stick) butter, softened
1 cup plus 2 tablespoons sugar
2 eggs
1 teaspoon pure vanilla extract

ICE CREAM BOMBE
1 1/2 pints of your first flavor of ice cream or sorbet, slightly softened
1 1/2 pints of your second flavor of ice cream or sorbet, slightly softened
1 tablespoon flour

MERINGUE
3 large egg whites, room temperature
Pinch of salt
3 tablespoons superfine sugar

CHOCOLATE CAKE: Preheat oven to 350 degrees.

Line the bottom of a 9-inch round cake pan with a round of parchment paper and spray with flour-based cooking spray.

In a small stainless bowl, pour water over cocoa and whisk until smooth. Let mixture cool. In another bowl, whisk together flour, baking soda, baking powder, and salt. Set aside.

In the bowl of an electric stand mixer, beat butter and sugar until fluffy then add eggs, one at a time, followed by vanilla. Beat in cocoa mixture and then slowly add flour mixture to combine.

Carefully pour batter into prepared cake pan. Bake until a toothpick inserted in the middle comes up clean, about 25 minutes. Remove from oven and let cool on a wire rack.

ICE CREAM BOMBE: Spray a 5-cup metal bowl (9 inches in diameter) with nonstick cooking spray; line with plastic wrap. Pack base of bowl with first flavor of ice cream; add second flavor on top. Pack firmly, cover surface with plastic wrap, and place in freezer. Freeze until ice cream is very hard, 2 hours or more.

Remove ice cream bombe from freezer and remove plastic wrap from top only. Working quickly, invert cooled cake onto base of ice cream bombe to create an ice cream cake. Cover cake surface with plastic wrap and return ice cream cake to freezer for another hour.

About a half hour before you want to serve the Baked Alaska, take ice cream-topped cake out of freezer. Invert onto a baking sheet. Lift bowl from top of cake to reveal ice cream dome. Remove plastic wrap. Working quickly, sift flour over the top and sides of ice cream (this will keep the meringue from sliding off of the dome.) Return to freezer while you make the meringue.

MERINGUE: Preheat oven to 500 degrees.

In the bowl of an electric stand mixer fitted with the whisk attachment, beat egg whites until foamy. Add salt and beat until soft peaks form. Add sugar and beat on high until peaks are stiff and glossy.

Note: If you are concerned about consuming raw eggs, you may use a Swiss or Italian method for the meringue instead.

TO ASSEMBLE BAKED ALASKA: Fill a pastry bag, fitted with a large star tip, with meringue. Take ice cream cake out of freezer and working very quickly, pipe meringue onto ice cream cake in a decorative fashion, or spoon meringue over ice cream cake and swirl with a rubber spatula.

Place meringue-topped ice cream cake in oven and bake until meringue becomes golden, for 4–5 minutes. Remove from oven and serve immediately.

Île Flottante with Salted Caramel and Toasted Hazelnuts

Serves 6–8

Île Flottante—French for "floating islands"—are incredibly light and unbelievably decadent at the same time. Soft meringues floating in a pool of sweet Crème Anglaise, this dessert can be served warm or chilled. We love it icy cold on a hot summer day, especially this version with the salted caramel and hazelnuts.

MERINGUE ISLANDS
4 egg whites, room temperature
   (reserve yolks to make Crème Anglaise)
$1/4$ teaspoon cream of tartar
Pinch of salt
$1/2$ cup superfine sugar
2 cups whole milk, or more, for poaching meringues
   (reserve leftover milk for Crème Anglaise)

CRÈME ANGLAISE
4 egg yolks
$1/2$ cup superfine sugar
1 teaspoon cornstarch
$1 3/4$ cups milk leftover from poaching meringues
   (add more milk if needed to make this amount)
2 teaspoons pure vanilla extract

SALTED CARAMEL SAUCE
2 cups firmly packed brown sugar
$1/4$ cup water
$1/2$ cup heavy cream, warmed
$1/4$ teaspoon sea salt

TOPPINGS
Sea salt
$1/2$ cup chopped toasted hazelnuts

MERINGUE ISLANDS: In the bowl of an electric stand mixer fitted with the whisk attachment, beat egg whites and cream of tartar until foamy. Add salt and beat on medium-high until they have soft peaks. Gradually add sugar, about a tablespoon at a time, and beat on high until stiff, glossy peaks form. Add vanilla and beat just until blended.

In a wide saucepan, heat milk to simmer, being careful not to boil. Using a large serving spoon, drop spoonfuls of meringue gently into milk. Poach meringue "islands" for 1 minute, fitting no more than 4 in the pan at a time, then turn over with a spoon and poach again, for another minute. Remove with a slotted spoon and place on a parchment paper-lined baking sheet.

If serving warm, place them into a warming drawer or oven at about 200 degrees. You may also refrigerate them if serving cold.

CRÈME ANGLAISE: Strain any eggy bits out of the warm milk; set aside.

In a clean bowl of an electric stand mixer fitted with the whisk attachment, beat egg yolks and sugar on medium for 3 minutes. Reduce speed to low, add cornstarch, and then gently add the reserved warm milk. Pour this mixture into a clean saucepan and cook over low heat. Stir with a long wooden spoon until thickened. Make sure to keep the heat low so that you don't scramble the eggs. When it's ready, the mixture will coat the back of a spoon. Add vanilla, stir, and then strain into a bowl. Chill if you are using later.

SALTED CARAMEL SAUCE: Combine the sugar and water in a large heavy-bottom saucepan over medium heat. Heat, swirling the pot around, until the mixture is a deep caramel color and looks like syrup, about 8 minutes. Carefully pour in the cream (it will bubble up) and continue to cook for another minute. Stir in salt. Cool to room temperature.

TO ASSEMBLE AND SERVE ÎLE FLOTTANTE: Place an "island" into individual pretty bowls or glasses. Spoon Crème Anglaise around the meringue. Drizzle caramel sauce over the top and sprinkle with sea salt and chopped hazelnuts.

Oeufs À La Neige
Au Fleur D'Oranger with Toasted Pistachios

Serves 6–8

There is much dialogue about the difference between Oeufs à la Neige (eggs in snow) and Île Flottante (floating islands). The ingredients and cooking methods are very similar, though Île Flottante is always served with a caramel sauce and one would imagine Oeufs à la Neige would be served icy cold.

MERINGUE OEUFS (EGGS)
4 egg whites, room temperature
   (reserve yolks for Crème Anglaise)
1/4 teaspoon cream of tartar
Pinch of kosher salt
1 cup superfine sugar
1 teaspoon pure vanilla extract
4 cups water

FLEUR D'ORANGER CRÈME ANGLAISE (SNOW)
1 cup milk
4 egg yolks
1/2 cup superfine sugar
1 teaspoon cornstarch
2 teaspoons fleur d'oranger water
   (available at gourmet food stores and online)

GARNISH
1/2 cup pistachios, lightly toasted

MERINGUE OEUFS: In the bowl of an electric stand mixer fitted with the whisk attachment, beat egg whites and cream of tartar on medium-high until soft peaks form. Add salt, then increase speed to high, and gradually add sugar, about a tablespoon at a time, until stiff, glossy peaks form. Add vanilla; beat just until blended.

In a wide saucepan, heat water to simmer. Be careful not to boil. Using a large serving spoon, drop spoonfuls of meringue gently into simmering water, fitting no more than 4 into a pan at once as they will expand when cooked. Poach each meringue for 1 minute, then turn over with a spoon and poach again, for another minute. Do not overcook.

Remove with a slotted spoon and place on a parchment paper-lined baking sheet. Place meringues into a warm oven or warming drawer at 200 degrees for about 5 minutes to dry. Transfer to refrigerator and chill until ready to serve.

FLEUR D'ORANGER CRÈME ANGLAISE: Warm milk in a saucepan. In a clean bowl with an electric mixer, beat the egg yolks and sugar on medium for 3 minutes. Reduce to low, add cornstarch and fleur d'oranger, then add the milk. Pour this mixture back into the pan and cook over low heat.

Stir with a long wooden spoon until thickened. Make sure to keep the heat low so that you don't scramble the eggs. When it's ready, the mixture will coat the back of a spoon. Strain into a bowl. Chill.

TO ASSEMBLE AND SERVE OEUFS À LA NEIGE: Divide Crème Anglaise among pretty individual bowls for serving. Top each with a meringue "egg." Sprinkle toasted pistachios lightly over the top and serve.

Raspberry Chambord Eton Mess

Serves 8

Eton Mess (named for Eton College) is one of Britain's favorite desserts and is literally a pile of broken up meringues folded into freshly whipped cream and berries. This is as close to the original version as you would want it, but the Chambord liqueur takes it over the top with its sweet raspberry essence.

4 cups raspberries, rinsed and dried
2 teaspoons sugar
2 teaspoons Chambord
2 cups heavy whipping cream
Approximately 12–16 Classic French Meringues (page 41)

Place berries in a bowl; add sugar and Chambord. Let stand for 30 minutes to release juices while you whip cream.

Whip the cream in a large bowl with an electric mixer until thick, but still soft. Roughly crumble in meringue cookies. You will need chunks for texture as well as a little fine dust. Fold in $3\frac{1}{2}$ cups of the raspberries.

Spoon onto 8 serving plates or into individual glass bowls and top each with some of the remaining raspberries.

Violet Macarons

Makes 24

There's something very special about a French *macaron*—that delicate almond meringue sandwich cookie that was created at Ladurée in Paris. We've tasted macarons in almost every flavor combination, but we think that this violet macaron with a creamy vanilla-violet filling is dreamy.

VIOLET MACARON COOKIES
1/2 cup blanched whole almonds
1 3/4 cups powdered sugar, divided
3 large egg whites, room temperature
Pinch of salt
2 tablespoons superfine sugar
1 teaspoon violet extract
1 or 2 scant drops violet food coloring

VANILLA-VIOLET BUTTERCREAM FILLING
1/2 cup (1 stick) unsalted butter, softened
3 cups powdered sugar
1 teaspoon pure vanilla extract
A few drops of violet extract
A few drops of violet food coloring
1 to 2 tablespoons milk or half-and-half

VIOLET MACARON COOKIES: Preheat oven to 325 degrees.

Pulse the almonds with 1 cup powdered sugar in a food processor until finely ground. Add remaining powdered sugar and pulse until well blended.

In the bowl of an electric stand mixer fitted with the whisk attachment, beat the egg whites until foamy. Add salt and beat on medium-high until soft peaks form. Add the superfine sugar, about a tablespoon at a time, and beat on high just until stiff peaks form. Add violet extract and food coloring and beat again for a few seconds to incorporate. With a rubber spatula, gently fold in the almond mixture.

Transfer the meringue to a pastry bag fitted with a 1/2-inch plain tip. Pipe out 48 mounds, 1 inch in diameter, about 2 inches apart on baking sheets lined with parchment paper. Bake, 1 sheet at a time, for 6–8 minutes, until the tops are cracked and appear dry but the macarons are still slightly soft to the touch.

Transfer the cookies, still on the parchment paper, to barely dampened kitchen towels and let cool for 5 minutes. Carefully peel the paper off the macarons and transfer to wire racks to completely cool.

VANILLA-VIOLET BUTTERCREAM FILLING: With an electric mixer, beat butter until fluffy then slowly add powdered sugar, beating until incorporated. Add vanilla and violet extracts and a few drops of food coloring, and beat again. Add a drizzle of milk until consistency is stiff, but creamy.

TO ASSEMBLE MACARONS: Fill a pastry bag with the buttercream filling. Turn macarons so their flat bottoms face up. On half of them, pipe about 1 teaspoon filling. Sandwich these with the remaining macarons, flat side down, pressing slightly to spread the filling to the edges. Refrigerate until firm, about 1 hour. Store in an airtight container in the refrigerator for up to a week.

Tiramisu with Espresso Meringue Ladyfingers

Serves 8–10

Layered with espresso-flavored meringue "ladyfingers" and made without raw egg yolk, our lighter version of this popular dessert has all the wonderful flavors of a traditional Tiramisu.

MERINGUE
4 large egg whites, room temperature
¼ teaspoon cream of tartar
¼ cup powdered sugar
¾ cup superfine sugar
½ teaspoon ground espresso

TIRAMISU FILLING
2 cups heavy whipping cream
5 tablespoons powdered sugar
8 ounces mascarpone cheese, room temperature
½ cup sugar
3 tablespoons Marsala wine or substitute dark rum,
   Madeira, port, brandy, cognac, or espresso

TO ASSEMBLE TIRAMISU
1 cup espresso (or strong coffee), cooled
3 tablespoons unsweetened cocoa powder

MERINGUE: Preheat oven to 200 degrees.

In the bowl of an electric stand mixer fitted with the whisk attachment, beat egg whites and cream of tartar on medium-high speed until soft peaks form. Gradually add powdered sugar, followed by the superfine sugar, about a tablespoon at a time. Scrape down sides of bowl, if needed. Increase speed to high and continue beating until stiff, glossy peaks form. Add espresso and beat just until incorporated.

Spoon meringue into a gallon-size ziplock bag. Seal the bag securely then, with scissors, snip off one bottom corner of the bag, 1 inch across. Pipe 24 (4-inch long) meringue ladyfingers onto baking sheets lined with parchment paper, about 1 inch apart. Bake for 90 minutes. Turn off heat and leave meringues in the oven for 1 additional hour to crisp. Cool completely before removing from baking sheet.

TIRAMISU FILLING: In the bowl of an electric stand mixer fitted with the whisk attachment, whip the cream and powdered sugar on high until thick. Set aside.

In a separate bowl, beat the mascarpone cheese and sugar until light and fluffy. Add Marsala and beat until incorporated. Gently fold half of the whipped cream into the mascarpone mixture—keeping the other half to spread on top of the assembled Tiramisu.

TO ASSEMBLE TIRAMISU: One by one, quickly dip half the meringue ladyfingers into the espresso—don't let ladyfingers soak; you don't want them to get soggy. Place them side-by-side to cover the bottom of a 9 x 12-inch serving dish. Gently spread half of the mascarpone cream mixture over the ladyfingers then dust with a layer of cocoa powder. Repeat, with the remaining ladyfingers, mascarpone cream, and cocoa powder to form the second layer. Gently spread remaining whipped cream over the entire surface then dust with a final layer of cocoa powder. Cover and chill for 2 hours or more before serving.

Variation: If you are use a smaller serving dish, divide the ladyfingers and mascarpone cream mixture to create additional layers.

Praline Meringue Cups with Huckleberry Sauce

Makes 6

We recently sampled fresh huckleberries at our favorite gourmet store and were amazed at how the ripe, flavorful berries melted in our mouths. Since they are seasonal, we were happy to discover that frozen berries can be ordered online year round, though blackberries can easily be substituted in this dessert.

HUCKLEBERRY SAUCE
2 cups fresh wild huckleberries or 16 ounces frozen huckleberries, thawed
1 tablespoon sugar

MERINGUE CUPS
4 large egg whites, room temperature
1/4 teaspoon cream of tartar
1/4 cup firmly packed brown sugar

3/4 superfine sugar
1 tablespoon cornstarch
3 tablespoons English toffee bits

FILLING AND TOPPINGS
1/4 cup chopped toasted pecans
6 scoops high quality vanilla ice cream
1 pint fresh huckleberries

HUCKLEBERRY SAUCE: Macerate berries in sugar for 1 hour then purée them with their juices in food processor. Press through sieve to strain out seeds. Cover and refrigerate sauce until ready to serve.

MERINGUE CUPS: Preheat oven to 225 degrees. Trace 3 circles, each approximately 3 1/2 inches in diameter, on 2 pieces of parchment paper so that you have 6 circles in total. Place parchment, marked side down, on baking sheets.

In the bowl of an electric stand mixer fitted with the whisk attachment, beat egg whites and cream of tartar on medium-high until soft peaks form. Add brown sugar, followed by superfine sugar, about a tablespoon at a time, and beat on high until stiff, glossy peaks form. Beat in cornstarch until incorporated then fold in toffee bits.

Spoon meringue into a pastry bag fitted with large star tip. Starting in the center of one parchment sheet circle, pipe meringue in concentric circles to fill it completely. Then, form the raised sides of the meringue cup by piping another circle along the edge. Repeat with remaining circles.

Bake meringues for 90 minutes until firm and dry. Turn off oven; let meringue cups stand in closed oven 1 hour or more.

TO ASSEMBLE AND SERVE MERINGUE CUPS: Place meringue cups on individual dessert plates. Sprinkle chopped pecans inside each meringue cup and add a scoop of ice cream. Drizzle Huckleberry Sauce over each and garnish with fresh berries.

Celebrations

Any meal becomes a special occasion when meringue is served for dessert. Nevertheless, we couldn't help including some festive holiday recipes. After all, some of the best memories are made over holiday meals with family and friends. The recipes in this chapter were inspired by our favorite holiday sweets throughout the year.

Instead of your traditional pumpkin pie at Thanksgiving, or those iced sugar cookies at Christmas, why not whip up a batch of Pumpkin Praline Tartlets or snowy, striped peppermint Candy Cane Clouds instead? We hope the desserts in this chapter will inspire you to mark every occasion and celebration with meringue, and to begin some new holiday traditions of your own.

Valentine Passion Fruit Vacherins

Makes 8

We are in love. With passion fruit. Who wouldn't fall for this dessert of heart-shaped meringues filled with vanilla-bean ice cream and topped with passion fruit? Whether you're creating a romantic dessert for that special someone, or something special for a larger gathering of loved ones, this dessert is simple elegance at its best.

MERINGUE HEARTS
4 large egg whites, room temperature
1 teaspoon white wine vinegar
Pinch of salt
3/4 cup superfine sugar
1 teaspoon pure vanilla extract
2 teaspoons cornstarch

FILLING AND TOPPING
8 passion fruits
1 1/2 teaspoons sugar
1 quart vanilla-bean ice cream or vanilla frozen yogurt

MERINGUE HEARTS: Preheat oven to 350 degrees.

In the bowl of an electric stand mixer fitted with the whisk attachment, beat egg whites until foamy. Add vinegar and salt and continue beating on medium-high to soft peaks. Slowly add sugar, about a tablespoon at a time, beating on high until whites are stiff and shiny. Add vanilla then sprinkle cornstarch over meringue and beat until incorporated.

On parchment paper-lined baking sheets, pipe meringue into 8 heart-shapes, each one about 4 inches across at the widest point. (Note, unlike Pavlovas, these have no bottoms.) Continue to pipe, building meringue sides up to about 3 inches high. Place in oven and turn heat down immediately to 300 degrees. Bake 30 minutes and then turn oven off, leaving meringues in for an additional 30 minutes. Take out of the oven to cool.

FILLING AND TOPPING: Cut open passion fruits and scoop pulp into a bowl. Add sugar and stir.

TO ASSEMBLE AND SERVE VACHERINS: When ready to serve, place meringue hearts onto individual dessert plates. Fill the center of each heart with ice cream and top with sweetened passion fruit.

Irish Cream Sundae Parfaits

Makes 8

Embracing her Irish roots, Jennifer's mom has always loved Bailey's Irish Cream, and recently left a bottle at Jen's house. We couldn't resist cracking it open one night to create this delicious parfait of vanilla ice cream, crisp meringues, and Bailey's whipped cream. It's particularly delicious with Bailey's and warm fudge sauce drizzled over the top. May the luck of the Irish be with you.

1 quart vanilla ice cream
1/2 recipe, approximately 24,
   Classic French Meringues (page 41)
Warm Espresso Fudge Sauce, optional (page 125)

BAILEY'S WHIPPED CREAM
2 tablespoons Bailey's Irish Cream Liqueur,
   plus more for drizzling
1 cup heavy whipping cream
1 tablespoon sugar

BAILEY'S WHIPPED CREAM: Using an electric mixer, whip cream, Bailey's, and sugar until stiff.

TO ASSEMBLE AND SERVE PARFAITS: In 8 parfait glasses, layer a scoop of ice cream, 2 crumbled meringue cookies, and a generous dollop of Bailey's whipped cream. Top with a meringue cookie. Drizzle with Bailey's, and if using, warm fudge sauce. Serve immediately.

Passover Blackberry Pavlova

Serves 8–10

For years Linda has been making a Pavlova for Passover (Pesach), the Jewish holiday that usually falls during March or April commemorating the exodus of the ancient Israelites from slavery in Egypt. During this seven-day holiday, eating foods made with leavened grains is prohibited. Ashkenazi Jews (from Germany and Eastern Europe) don't allow corn products (hence, the potato starch option in this recipe) while Sephardic Jews (from Spain and the Mediterranean areas) do. Either way, this Blackberry Pavlova, with honey-sweetened whipped cream, is the perfect way to end the Passover Seder meal.

PAVLOVA SHELL
4 large egg whites, room temperature
1 teaspoon white vinegar
Pinch of salt
1 cup superfine sugar
1/4 teaspoon pure vanilla extract
1/8 teaspoon almond extract
1 teaspoon cornstarch or potato starch

HONEY WHIPPED CREAM
1 cup heavy whipping cream
3 tablespoons honey
1 teaspoon pure vanilla extract

FRUIT
3 cups fresh blackberries
2 tablespoons sugar

PAVLOVA SHELL: Preheat oven to 350 degrees.

In the bowl of an electric stand mixer fitted with the whisk attachment, beat egg whites until foamy. Increase speed to medium-high and add vinegar and salt; beat until soft peaks form. Add sugar, about a tablespoon at a time, beating on high, until meringue is glossy with stiff peaks. Beat in vanilla and almond extracts then cornstarch, about 1 minute more.

With a rubber spatula, place the meringue in the center of a baking sheet covered with parchment paper. Using the back of a spoon, spread the meringue to form a 10-inch shell, with sides higher than center. Bake for 5 minutes, then lower the temperature to 250 degrees and continue baking for 1 hour. Turn the heat off and leave the meringue shell in the oven for 3 hours or more (or overnight) so that it continues to dry and crisp. When completely cooled, loosen the meringue by gently peeling it off the parchment or by sliding an offset spatula or knife underneath the shell.

HONEY WHIPPED CREAM: With an electric mixer, whip cream on medium until it starts to thicken. Turn off mixer and add honey and vanilla. Resume beating, increasing speed to medium-high, until the whipped cream is stiff.

FRUIT: Rinse the fruit and allow to dry in a colander or on paper towels. Transfer to a bowl and gently toss with sugar.

TO ASSEMBLE PAVLOVA: Carefully transfer the meringue shell to a large, flat serving plate. Don't be alarmed if the edges of the shell crack a bit and some pieces break off. Spread whipped cream filling on meringue shell, leaving about a 1-inch border from the edge. Top with the blackberries.

Coconut Meringue Nests with Raspberry Curd

Makes 8

Coconut and chocolate are two of the flavors we always associate with Easter, so we were inspired to create these darling coconut meringue nests. Filled with bright raspberry curd and topped with whipped cream and shaved bittersweet chocolate, they make a lovely, festive holiday dessert.

COCONUT MERINGUE NESTS
4 large egg whites, room temperature (reserve yolks for curd)
1 teaspoon white vinegar
Pinch of salt
1 cup superfine sugar
1 teaspoon cornstarch
1 cup unsweetened shredded coconut

RASPBERRY CURD
6 egg yolks, lightly beaten
1 pint fresh raspberries or a 12-ounce bag of frozen, thawed
1/2 cup (1 stick) unsalted butter, cut into 1/2-inch pieces
1 cup sugar
1/4 teaspoon kosher salt
3 tablespoons fresh lemon juice

WHIPPED CREAM TOPPING AND GARNISH
1 cup heavy whipping cream
2 tablespoons powdered sugar
1/2 teaspoon pure vanilla extract
Shaved bittersweet chocolate

COCONUT MERINGUE NESTS: Preheat oven to 350 degrees.

In the bowl of an electric stand mixer fitted with the whisk attachment, beat egg whites until foamy. Add vinegar and salt and continue to beat on medium-high until soft peaks form. Gradually add the sugar, about a tablespoon at a time, beating on high until meringue has stiff, glossy peaks. Add cornstarch, beat until incorporated, and then beat in coconut.

On baking sheets lined with parchment paper, form 8 meringue nests, approximately 4 inches in diameter, by using the back of a spoon to spread the meringue from the center out to the sides, building up the sides to about 1 inch high. Bake for 5 minutes then reduce heat to 250 degrees and bake for 1 hour. Turn off heat and leave meringues in the oven for 1 additional hour or more to dry. Cool completely before removing from baking sheets. Nests can be made a day or two in advance and stored in an airtight container.

RASPBERRY CURD: Combine all of the ingredients in a cold medium saucepan. Turn heat to medium-high and cook, stirring constantly with a wooden spoon—mashing the raspberries as you stir—until the mixture is thick enough to coat the back of a spoon, about 10 minutes.

To remove the seeds, pour the curd through a mesh colander or sieve placed over a bowl. If some of the seeds slip through, repeat this step. Cover with plastic wrap and chill until ready to use.

Note: The curd can be made a week in advance and stored in an airtight container in the refrigerator.

WHIPPED CREAM TOPPING: With an electric mixer, whip cream, sugar, and vanilla until stiff.

TO ASSEMBLE AND SERVE NESTS: Place meringue nests on individual dessert plates. Spoon about 2 tablespoons of the Raspberry Curd in the middle of each nest. Top with a dollop of whipped cream and sprinkle with shaved bittersweet chocolate.

Red, White, and Blueberry Trifle

Serves 8–10

Alternating layers of brilliant white meringues, creamy vanilla pudding, blueberries, whipped cream, and juicy red strawberries make for a colorful dessert that's perfect for Memorial Day, the Fourth of July, and Labor Day. Serve it in a glass trifle bowl to showcase all the gorgeous layers. And to really get into the holiday spirit, add a few long, sparkler candles on top.

MERINGUE COOKIES
Approximately 48 Classic French Meringues (page 41)

VANILLA PUDDING
3 tablespoons cornstarch
2 1/2 cups whole milk, divided
2/3 cup sugar
1/8 teaspoon salt
2 teaspoons pure vanilla extract
1 tablespoon unsalted butter, softened

WHIPPED CREAM
1 1/2 cups heavy whipping cream
3 tablespoons powdered sugar

FRUIT
2 pints fresh blueberries, rinsed and dried
2 pints fresh strawberries, rinsed, dried, hulled, and sliced

VANILLA PUDDING: In a small bowl, add cornstarch to 1/2 cup milk and stir until blended and no lumps remain. Set aside.

In a medium saucepan, heat the remaining milk, sugar, and salt over medium-low. Cook just until it starts to steam and very tiny bubbles begin to form around the edge of the pan; increase temperature to medium.

Red, White, and Blueberry Trifle (continued)

Give the milk and cornstarch mixture another stir to incorporate any of the cornstarch that may have settled at the bottom then pour into the pan of heated milk. Cook, stirring occasionally, until mixture starts to thicken and just begins to boil. Immediately reduce the heat to the lowest setting and stir continually for about 5 minutes, until thick. Add the vanilla, then the butter, and stir until it has melted into the pudding.

Remove from heat and pour into a medium-size bowl and cover the entire surface with plastic wrap to prevent the pudding from forming a skin. Refrigerate 4 hours or more.

WHIPPED CREAM: In the bowl of an electric stand mixer fitted with the whisk attachment, beat cream and sugar until stiff.

TO ASSEMBLE TRIFLE: Place 20 of the meringue cookies on the bottom of a 12-cup trifle dish. Layer with half of the vanilla pudding, then half of the blueberries, followed by half of the whipped cream, topped with half of the strawberries. Repeat, starting with meringues and ending up with the strawberries on top. Cover with plastic wrap and refrigerate for 1 hour or more. Decorate the top with the remaining meringue cookies before serving.

Variation: To make individual servings, layer the meringues, pudding, berries, and whipped cream in glass bowls or Mason jars.

Meringue Ghosts

Makes about 12

Even though our kids are getting into their teen years, they still love Halloween, and love helping make these adorable not-so-spooky ghosts with their pure white meringue bodies and candy eyes. Displayed on a plate, they make a great holiday decoration and a delicious treat.

2 large egg whites, room temperature
Pinch of cream of tartar
Pinch of salt
3/4 cup sifted powdered sugar
24 edible silver balls or mini chocolate chips

Preheat oven to 200 degrees.

Place the egg whites and cream of tartar in the bowl of an electric stand mixer fitted with the whisk attachment; beat on medium-high until soft peaks form. Add the salt then the sugar, about a tablespoon at a time, beating on high until you have stiff, glossy peaks.

Fill a pastry bag fitted with a 1/2-inch round tip with meringue. On baking sheets lined with parchment paper, create ghosts by piping a circle about 1 1/2–2 inches in diameter then make spirals all the way up, making them smaller as you get to the ghost's head. The finished ghost will be approximately 3 inches high. Carefully press the candy balls or chocolate chips onto each ghost, creating eyes. Alternatively, you can create eyes by piping melted chocolate onto the ghosts once they are baked and completely cooled.

Bake for 1 hour, then prop oven door open with a wooden spoon and bake 30 minutes more. Turn off the oven and leave the ghosts inside until they have completely dried and come to room temperature. The ghosts can be kept in a sealed container for up to a week.

Pumpkin Praline Tartlets

Makes 8

This is a fabulous alternative to a traditional Thanksgiving pumpkin pie. Individual brown sugar meringue shells are filled with Pumpkin Mousse and topped with a dollop of whipped cream and a generous sprinkling of pecan Praline Crumble. After eating all that turkey, everyone will appreciate this wonderfully light dessert.

MERINGUE TARTLET SHELLS
4 large egg whites, room temperature
1 teaspoon white vinegar
Pinch of salt
2/3 cup superfine sugar
1/3 cup firmly packed brown sugar
1 teaspoon cornstarch

PUMPKIN MOUSSE AND WHIPPED CREAM TOPPING
1 cup of canned pumpkin purée
2 cups heavy whipping cream, divided
1/3 cup sugar
1/2 teaspoon ground cinnamon
1/4 teaspoon ground ginger
1/8 teaspoon ground nutmeg
3 tablespoons powdered sugar
1 teaspoon pure vanilla extract

PRALINE CRUMBLE TOPPING
1/2 cup sugar
1/3 cup water
1/2 cup chopped pecans
Pinch of kosher salt

MERINGUE TARTLET SHELLS: Preheat oven to 350 degrees.

In the bowl of an electric stand mixer fitted with the whisk attachment, beat egg whites until foamy. Increase speed to medium-high and add vinegar and salt; continue to beat until soft peaks form. Gradually add the sugars, about a tablespoon at a time, beating on high until stiff, glossy peaks form. Add cornstarch and beat until incorporated.

On baking sheets lined with parchment paper, form 8 meringue tartlet shells, approximately 5 inches in diameter by using the back of a spoon to spread the meringue from the center out to the sides, building up the sides to about 1 inch high. Or, if you prefer, you can use a pastry bag and decorative tip to pipe them. Bake for 5 minutes, then reduce heat to 250 degrees and bake for 1 hour. Turn off heat and leave meringues in the oven for 1 additional hour or more to dry. Cool completely before removing from baking sheets.

PUMPKIN MOUSSE AND WHIPPED CREAM TOPPING: In a medium saucepan, combine pumpkin, $1/2$ cup cream, sugar, and spices. Bring to a simmer over medium heat and cook, stirring occasionally, for 5 minutes. Transfer to a medium bowl and set aside to cool completely.

With an electric mixer, whip remaining cream, powdered sugar, and vanilla until it is thick and forms soft peaks. Fold approximately two-thirds of the whipped cream into the pumpkin mixture until no large streaks of pumpkin or cream remain. Place the Pumpkin Mouse and remaining whipped cream in the refrigerator until ready to use.

PRALINE CRUMBLE TOPPING: Line a baking sheet with foil or a silicone mat. Spray a rubber spatula with non-stick cooking spray to prevent hot praline mixture from sticking and set aside.

In a small, heavy-bottom saucepan, bring sugar and water to a simmer over medium heat, stirring occasionally. When the sugar has dissolved, increase heat to medium-high and continue cooking, without stirring, until the sugar syrup turns a medium amber color. Watch it carefully to make sure it doesn't get too dark and burns. Remove from heat and stir in pecans and salt. Immediately pour praline mixture onto prepared baking sheet and, with rubber spatula, spread into a thin layer. When it has cooled, break the praline into small pieces. You can prepare this up to a week ahead and store in an airtight container.

TO ASSEMBLE TARTLETS: Place meringue tartlet shells on individual dessert plates. Divide Pumpkin Mousse evenly among the shells. (Refrigerate any leftover mousse.) Top with a dollop of the whipped cream and generously sprinkle with Praline Crumble Topping.

Hanukkah Lights

Makes about 36

The sparkling blue sugar atop the white meringue cookies reflects the traditional Hanukkah colors and reminds us of the flickering light of the menorah candles. For a sweet little hostess gift or party favor, Linda likes to tuck a few inside a clear cellophane bag tied with a silver satin ribbon.

3 large egg whites, room temperature
1/8 teaspoon cream of tartar
3/4 cup superfine sugar
1/2 teaspoon pure vanilla extract
2 tablespoons blue sanding sugar, divided

Preheat oven to 200 degrees.

In the bowl of an electric stand mixer fitted with the whisk attachment, beat egg whites and cream of tartar on medium-high speed until soft peaks form. Gradually add sugar, about a tablespoon at a time, beating on high until stiff, glossy peaks form. Add vanilla and 1 tablespoon of the sanding sugar and beat just until incorporated.

Transfer meringue to a pastry bag fitted with a large star tip and pipe onto baking sheets covered with parchment paper, about 1 inch apart. Sprinkle remaining sanding sugar on top of each cookie. Bake for 90 minutes. Turn off heat and leave meringues in the oven for 1 additional hour or more to dry. Cool completely before removing from baking sheets.

Candy Cane Clouds

Makes about 30

These delicate red and white striped meringues remind us of candy canes on Christmas morning. Have plenty of these cloud-like cookies sitting in pretty candy dishes to serve when friends drop by.

3 large egg whites, room temperature
1/8 teaspoon cream of tartar
3/4 cup powdered sugar
3/4 teaspoon peppermint extract
  (or more if you prefer a stronger mint taste)
Red gel paste food coloring (do not substitute liquid food coloring)

Preheat oven to 200 degrees.

In the bowl of an electric stand mixer fitted with the whisk attachment, beat egg whites and cream of tartar on medium-high until soft peaks form. Reduce speed to medium and add powdered sugar, about a tablespoon at a time. When all the sugar has been added, stop the mixer and gently scrape down the sides of the bowl with a rubber spatula since the powdered sugar tends to fly up and cling to the sides. Turn mixer back on and continue beating on high until stiff, glossy peaks form. Mix in peppermint extract.

To create the candy cane stripes, you'll need a pastry bag fitted with a large open star tip and a small, clean fine-tipped paintbrush. Along the inside of the star tip, paint 4–5 thin red food coloring stripes spaced evenly apart. Fill the bag with half of the meringue and pipe cookies onto parchment-lined baking sheets. As the meringue moves through the tip, it picks up the red stripes.

When the bag is empty, remove the star tip from the couplet and wipe off the inside of the tip. Repaint the stripes, reattach the tip, add the rest of the meringue to the pastry bag and continue piping. Bake for 90 minutes. Turn off heat and leave meringues in the oven for 1 additional hour or more to dry. Cool completely before carefully removing from baking sheets.

Meringue Bûche De Noël

Serves 12

A traditional Bûche de Noël (French for "Christmas Log") is decorated with charming meringue mushrooms. Our version does as well, but adds a new twist by replacing the traditional Genoise cake with a soft-baked chocolate meringue. Filled with chocolate-flecked chocolate whipped cream and covered with a dark chocolate ganache, you'll want to make this decadent, yet light Meringue Bûche de Noël your new Yuletide tradition.

MERINGUE MUSHROOMS (PAGE 63) MADE IN ADVANCE

MERINGUE CAKE
8 large egg whites, room temperature
1 tablespoon white vinegar
1 1/2 cups superfine sugar
1 teaspoon pure vanilla extract
2 tablespoons cornstarch
1/4 cup unsweetened cocoa powder

CHOCOLATE-FLECKED CHOCOLATE WHIPPED CREAM
1 cup heavy whipping cream
3 tablespoons powdered sugar
1 teaspoon pure vanilla extract
1 tablespoon unsweetened cocoa powder
1/2 cup coarsely chopped bittersweet chocolate

GANACHE
1/2 cup heavy whipping cream
6 ounces bittersweet or semisweet chocolate, chopped
2 tablespoons light corn syrup
1 teaspoon Grand Marnier, dark rum, or pure vanilla extract

MERINGUE CAKE: Preheat oven to 325 degrees.

Line a 10 x 15-inch jelly roll pan with parchment paper, lightly coated with nonstick cooking spray.

In the bowl of an electric stand mixer fitted with the whisk attachment, beat egg whites on medium-high until soft peaks form. Add the vinegar then the sugar, about a tablespoon at a time, and continue beating on high until you have stiff, glossy peaks. Reduce speed to medium and add vanilla, beating until incorporated. Add cornstarch, then cocoa powder, and beat; scrape down the sides of the bowl with a rubber spatula and continue beating just until the cocoa powder is incorporated.

With your spatula, spread meringue evenly in prepared jelly roll pan. Bake, rotating pan halfway through, 20–22 minutes, until the meringue is puffed. Remove from oven and cool in the pan on a wire rack.

CHOCOLATE-FLECKED CHOCOLATE WHIPPED CREAM: With an electric mixer, whip the cream, powdered sugar, and vanilla until thick but not yet stiff. Add cocoa powder and continue whipping until combined and no streaks of white remain then fold in chopped bittersweet chocolate.

GANACHE: Bring cream to simmer over medium heat in heavy-bottom saucepan. Do not boil. Remove from heat and add chocolate, corn syrup, and liqueur. Stir until mixture is smooth. Let the Ganache stand until it is thick and has reached room temperature. Place the pan in the refrigerator for about 15 minutes to thicken a bit more while you assemble the rest of the dessert.

TO ASSEMBLE AND SERVE THE BÛCHE DE NOËL: Invert the meringue cake onto a work surface. It should release very easily from the parchment paper, but in case it doesn't, run a knife just underneath the edges along all sides. Working with longer side of meringue facing you, spread the chocolate whipped cream evenly across the meringue, leaving a 1-inch border. Starting with the side nearest to you, gently roll the cream topped meringue into a log. The meringue may crack a bit when you roll it, but don't worry; that just makes it look all the more like tree bark, plus it will eventually be covered in ganache.

On a diagonal, slice about 3 inches off one of the ends. Carefully transfer the longer piece to your serving platter, seam side down then place the shorter piece with the diagonal cut side touching the side of the log so that it looks like a branch. Refrigerate, covered, for at least 1 hour.

With a silicone pastry brush or metal spatula, spread the Ganache over the top and sides of the Meringue Bûche de Noël, leaving the cut sides exposed so that the rings of meringue and cream show. To create the appearance of bark, lightly run the tines of a fork down the entire length of the Bûche in a slightly wavy pattern. You can also use a decorative tip to pipe the Ganache. Return to refrigerator, uncovered.

When you're ready to serve, dust lightly with powdered sugar to look like snow, if desired. Decorate by leaning some of the Meringue Mushrooms against the Bûche de Noël and by placing others around the serving platter.

Croquembouche

Serves 12

Traditionally a French wedding cake, somehow the Croquembouche, a tower of cream-filled profiteroles drizzled with caramel, became popular around the holidays. Jennifer has always loved making a Christmas Croquembouche, and we loved the idea of creating a version with meringues. The thin caramel spun around it glitters like gold, making it an elegant centerpiece for a holiday party. The trick is not to crumble the meringues while building the tower.

MERINGUE COOKIES
**Approximately 80 Classic French Meringues
(page 41, recipe doubled)**

SPECIAL SUPPLIES
**18-inch tall Styrofoam cone
(available at floral shops and craft stores)
Parchment paper, aluminum foil, or Martha Wrap
(foil and parchment in one), to cover cone**

SPUN CARAMEL
**1 cup sugar
1/2 cup plus 4 tablespoons water**

TIP: When working with caramel or spun sugar, keep a bowl of ice water nearby. Caramel burns are the worst, so if you wind up getting one, plunge affected area into water to stop from burning.

Place sugar in a medium saucepan and pour 1/2 cup water over it. Cover and cook over medium heat, without stirring, so that the sugar will not crystallize. Check it, and once it's boiling, leave cover off and watch it. When it turns just golden brown, take it off the heat and add remaining water. BE CAREFUL, the caramel will sizzle and spit for a few seconds. Swirl around, but do not stir. When the caramel has the consistency of maple syrup, remove from heat. You will need to work quickly and carefully at this point as the caramel will soon begin to harden.

TO ASSEMBLE CROQUEMBOUCHE: Using caramel as glue, and with a toothpick, dab a bit of caramel onto the back of meringue cookies, one at a time, and arrange around the bottom of the base. Continue to cover the cone with meringues, being careful not to crush them as you go. Place them closely together so there are no large gaps.

Once the entire cone is covered in meringues, using a spoon, swirl to spin thin strands of the remaining caramel all over the meringue-covered cone. If caramel hardens while you're still assembling the Croquembouche, put the pan back on low heat to liquefy it again. If you don't have enough caramel to cover all the cookies, make another small batch with $1/4$ cup sugar and 1 teaspoon water.

To add some extra holiday cheer, you may also decorate the Croquembouche with festive candy and holly leaves. Of course, the Croquembouche isn't just a pretty centerpiece; it's to be eaten! Simply pull the caramel covered meringues off of the cone and enjoy.

Little Clouds

When we were children, we watched our mothers whip up soft, fluffy meringues for their lemon pies, marveling at the sheer magic of egg whites and sugar becoming sweet, snowy clouds before our very eyes. Until now, it's been our little secret that meringues are deceptively simple to make, but they truly are so easy that even a child can make them. In fact, children as young as 5 years old make desserts such as Pavlovas and French Macarons in Jennifer's cooking classes in Los Angeles, and our own children love helping us make meringues as well.

While little ones will undoubtedly love eating and helping make most of the recipes in this book, we wanted to create a special chapter just for them. However, you needn't be a child or have a child, for that matter, to enjoy this chapter. Based on our own childhood favorite sweets, recipes such as S'moringues and Snowballs are bound to be a hit with anyone under the age of 100.

S'moringues

S'mores. Is there a more classic campfire treat? The name alone evokes vivid memories of marshmallows toasting on skewers over an open flame, sandwiched between Hershey's milk chocolate bars and graham crackers. In their honor, Linda and her kids created S'moringues, sweet little cookies with all the tastes of the original ingredients mixed in, but with meringue substituting for the marshmallows.

3 large egg whites, room temperature
1/8 teaspoon cream of tartar
3/4 cup superfine sugar
1/2 cup graham cracker crumbs
(about 3 1/2 graham cracker rectangles or 7 squares in food processor)
1 cup coarsely chopped milk chocolate (from 3 Hershey's 1.55-ounce bars)

Preheat oven to 200 degrees.

In the bowl of an electric stand mixer fitted with the whisk attachment, beat egg whites and cream of tartar on medium-high speed until soft peaks form. Increase speed to high and gradually add sugar, about a tablespoon at a time, beating until meringue is stiff, with glossy peaks. Gently fold in graham cracker crumbs and chocolate pieces.

Drop by well-rounded teaspoons onto baking sheets lined with parchment paper, about 1 inch apart. Bake for 90 minutes. Turn off heat and leave meringues in the oven for 1 additional hour to dry. Cool completely before removing from baking sheet.

Meringue Pizza

Makes 4

A meringue "crust" topped with raspberry curd "sauce," whipped cream and white chocolate "cheese," green-colored sweetened shredded coconut "basil," and sliced strawberry "pepperoni." This truly is food art, and kids love customizing their own individual dessert "pizza."

MERINGUE CRUST
2 large egg whites, room temperature
Pinch of salt
1/4 cup superfine sugar
1/4 cup firmly packed brown sugar

WHIPPED CREAM
1/2 cup heavy whipping cream
1 tablespoon powdered sugar

TOPPINGS
1/2 cup Raspberry Curd (page 186) or substitute Raspberry or Strawberry Jam
1/3 cup white chocolate chips or chopped white chocolate
1 tablespoon sweetened shredded coconut, mixed with a few drops of green food coloring
4 strawberries, sliced horizontally

MERINGUE CRUST: Preheat oven to 200 degrees.

In the bowl of a standing electric mixer fitted with the whisk attachment, beat egg whites until foamy. Add salt and continue beating on medium-high speed until soft peaks form. Reduce speed to low and add sugars, about a tablespoon at a time. When all the sugar has been added, stop the mixer for a moment to scrape down the sides of the bowl to make sure that all of the sugar has been incorporated. Resume beating on high until stiff, glossy peaks form.

On baking sheets lined with parchment paper, create 4 circles, approximately 5 1/2 inches in diameter, using the back of a spoon to spread the meringue. The outer edges should be raised slightly. Bake for 90 minutes, then turn off heat and leave in the oven for 1 hour to continue drying.

WHIPPED CREAM: With an electric mixer, whip cream and sugar until stiff.

TO ASSEMBLE "PIZZAS": Place meringue crusts on individual plates. Spread 1–2 tablespoons of raspberry curd on the surface of the meringue, leaving about a 1/2-inch border. Place dollops of whipped cream on top of the curd. Sprinkle white chocolate on top, add a few strawberry slices, then garnish with a bit of the green coconut.

Apple Cinnamon Nests

Makes 10

There is nothing like warm apple pie on a crisp fall day with the smell of cinnamon in the air. These sweet cinnamon nests filled with caramelized cinnamon apples and fluffy whipped cream taste just like apple pie on a cloud.

CINNAMON MERINGUE NESTS
8 large egg whites, room temperature
2 teaspoons white vinegar
Pinch of salt
1 1/2 cups superfine sugar
1/2 teaspoon pure vanilla extract
1 1/2 teaspoons cinnamon
4 teaspoons cornstarch

WHIPPED CREAM
2 cups heavy whipping cream

2–3 tablespoons sugar, or to taste
1 teaspoon pure vanilla extract

CARAMELIZED CINNAMON APPLES
6 tablespoons unsalted butter
6 apples (Pink Lady or Honeycrisp), peeled, cored, and thinly sliced
1/4 cup firmly packed light brown sugar
1/2 teaspoon cinnamon

CINNAMON MERINGUE NESTS: Preheat oven to 350 degrees.

In the bowl of an electric stand mixer fitted with the whisk attachment, beat egg whites until foamy. Add vinegar and salt and continue beating on medium-high speed to soft peaks. Slowly add sugar, about a tablespoon at a time, then increase speed to high and beat until whites are stiff and shiny. Add vanilla and cinnamon then sprinkle cornstarch over meringue and beat until incorporated.

On baking sheets lined with parchment paper, pipe or spoon meringue into 10 circles about 4 inches in diameter, making sides higher than the center. Place in oven and turn heat down immediately to 300 degrees. Bake 30 minutes and then turn oven off, leaving meringues in for an additional 30 minutes. Take out of the oven to cool.

WHIPPED CREAM: With an electric stand mixer, beat cream, sugar, and vanilla until you have stiff peaks. Chill until ready to assemble nests.

CARAMELIZED CINNAMON APPLES: Melt butter in a skillet. Add apples and then sprinkle sugar and cinnamon over the top. Cook over medium heat, stirring occasionally, until caramel-colored and very tender, about 20 minutes, depending on the type of apples you are using.

TO ASSEMBLE AND SERVE NESTS: Place cinnamon nests onto individual dessert plates. Fill with whipped cream, top with warm apples, and serve.

Chocolate Kisses

Makes 36

Hidden inside each of these decadent meringue cookies is a chocolate kiss surprise, which makes them a hit with children and grown-ups alike. After all, who wouldn't love a little kiss . . . or two?

3 large egg whites, room temperature
1/4 teaspoon cream of tartar
3/4 cup superfine sugar
1/4 teaspoon almond extract
1/8 teaspoon pure vanilla extract
36 milk chocolate kisses
Unsweetened cocoa powder

Preheat oven to 200 degrees.

In the bowl of an electric stand mixer fitted with the whisk attachment, beat egg whites and cream of tartar on medium-high speed until soft peaks form. Gradually add sugar, about a tablespoon at a time, beating on high speed until meringue is glossy with stiff peaks. Add almond extract and vanilla and beat until incorporated, about 1 minute more.

Line baking sheets with parchment paper. Gently spoon meringue into a pastry bag fitted with a medium-size star or round tip. Holding your pastry bag at a 90-degree angle to your baking sheets, pipe 36 shallow discs (about 1¼ inches in diameter) to form the base for your cookies. Lightly press one chocolate kiss into each meringue round. Pipe meringue in concentric circles, starting at the base and working toward the top, until the chocolate kiss is completely covered. Turn your baking sheets to look at the meringues from other angles to make sure the chocolate kisses are completely covered. Lightly dust with cocoa powder.

Bake for 90 minutes. Turn oven off and leave the meringues in the oven to dry, 1 hour or more. Remove from oven and cool completely before removing from baking sheets.

Death by Milk Chocolate

Makes 8

We're not in the least bit ashamed to admit we never outgrew our love for milk chocolate. So we created these parfaits, with layer after layer of milk chocolate in different forms and textures: Crisp and chewy meringues, smooth pudding, and fluffy chocolate whipped cream with the added crunch of milk chocolate chips. They let kids, young and old, indulge in milk chocolate to their hearts' delight.

CRUNCHY CHEWY CHOCOLATE MERINGUES
1/2 cup plus 2 tablespoons superfine sugar
1 1/2 teaspoons cornstarch
2 large egg whites, room temperature (reserve the yolks for pudding)
A pinch of salt
2 tablespoons unsweetened cocoa powder
1/4 teaspoon pure vanilla extract

MILK CHOCOLATE PUDDING
1/4 cup sugar
2 tablespoons plus 1 1/2 teaspoons unsweetened cocoa powder
1 tablespoon cornstarch
1 1/2 cups plus 2 tablespoons whole milk
2 large egg yolks
1 large egg
1/2 cup milk chocolate chips
1 tablespoon unsalted butter
3/4 teaspoon pure vanilla extract

CHOCOLATE–CHOCOLATE CHIP WHIPPED CREAM
1 cup heavy whipping cream
3 tablespoons powdered sugar
1 teaspoon pure vanilla extract
2 tablespoons unsweetened cocoa powder
1 cup milk chocolate chips

CRUNCHY CHEWY CHOCOLATE MERINGUES: Preheat oven to 275 degrees.

In a small bowl, whisk together sugar and cornstarch; set aside.

In the bowl of an electric stand mixer fitted with the whisk attachment, beat egg whites until foamy.

Add salt and continue beating on medium-high speed until soft peaks form. Decrease speed to medium and gradually add sugar mixture, about a tablespoon at a time. When all the sugar is incorporated, increase speed to high and beat until meringue is glossy with stiff peaks. Reduce speed to low and add cocoa powder, 1 tablespoon at a time, followed by vanilla; beat until no streaks of cocoa remain.

Drop by 16 large, rounded tablespoons onto baking sheets lined with parchment paper. Bake for 30 minutes. Turn heat off and leave cookies in the oven for an additional 30 minutes.

MILK CHOCOLATE PUDDING: In a medium saucepan, whisk together sugar, cocoa powder, and cornstarch; gradually whisk in milk. Over medium-high heat, whisk the mixture until it boils and has thickened slightly. Remove from heat and set aside.

In a large bowl, whisk egg yolks and egg. Gradually whisk in about half of the hot cocoa mixture so that the eggs don't curdle. Pour the egg and cocoa mixture back into the saucepan with the remaining hot cocoa mixture; return saucepan to stove and continue whisking over medium heat until mixture thickens, making sure it doesn't boil, about 5 minutes. Remove pan from the heat and add the chocolate chips, butter, and vanilla, and whisk until the pudding is smooth.

Transfer to a container or bowl. Place a sheet of plastic wrap directly on the surface of the pudding and refrigerate until ready to assemble parfaits. Pudding can be made a day in advance.

CHOCOLATE–CHOCOLATE CHIP WHIPPED CREAM: In the bowl of your electric stand mixer fitted with the whisk attachment, combine the cream, powdered sugar, and vanilla; whip until firm. Add cocoa powder and continue whipping until incorporated. Fold in chocolate chips.

TO ASSEMBLE PARFAITS: Place one broken meringue into the bottom of each of 8 parfait glasses or dessert bowls. Add a layer of pudding. Top with another broken meringue. Finish with Chocolate–Chocolate Chip Whipped Cream.

Very Vanilla Cups

Makes 8

Kids of all ages love vanilla, and these darling mini-vacherins will win the hearts of even the most dedicated chocolate lovers.

4 large egg whites, room temperature
1 teaspoon white vinegar
Pinch of salt
³/4 cup superfine sugar
2 teaspoons pure vanilla extract
2 teaspoons cornstarch
1 quart vanilla-bean ice cream, slightly softened

Preheat oven to 350 degrees.

In the bowl of an electric stand mixer fitted with the whisk attachment, beat egg whites until foamy. Increase speed to medium-high, add vinegar, then salt, and continue beating until soft peaks form. Slowly add sugar, about a tablespoon at a time, and increase speed to high and continue to beat until whites are stiff and shiny. Add vanilla then sprinkle cornstarch over whites and beat until incorporated.

Spoon meringue into a pastry bag fitted with a round 1/2-inch tip. On a parchment paper-lined baking sheet, pipe meringue into 8 cups about 4 inches in diameter, making sides higher than centers. Place in oven and turn heat down immediately to 275 degrees. Bake 30 minutes and then turn oven off, leaving meringues in for an additional 30 minutes. Take out of the oven to cool.

TO ASSEMBLE AND SERVE VERY VANILLA CUPS: Place meringue cups on individual plates. Spoon softened vanilla ice cream into cups. Enjoy immediately!

Snowballs

Makes 8

No one ever outgrows making snowballs, and in this recipe, we can all indulge by rolling sweet frosty balls of ice cream into crushed white meringue cookies.

1 quart coconut ice cream or sorbet
2 cups crumbled Classic French Meringues (page 41)

Line a baking sheet with parchment paper. Scoop the ice cream into 8 balls, place on the sheet, and freeze until firm, 8–10 minutes.

Place crumbled meringue in shallow bowl. Roll ice cream balls in meringue crumbles, pressing gently to help it adhere. If not serving immediately, return to freezer in an airtight container.

Index

Metric Conversion Chart

VOLUME MEASUREMENTS		WEIGHT MEASUREMENTS		TEMPERATURE CONVERSION	
U.S.	METRIC	U.S.	METRIC	FAHRENHEIT	CELSIUS
1 teaspoon	5 ml	1/2 ounce	15 g	250	120
1 tablespoon	15 ml	1 ounce	30 g	300	150
1/4 cup	60 ml	3 ounces	90 g	325	160
1/3 cup	75 ml	4 ounces	115 g	350	180
1/2 cup	125 ml	8 ounces	225 g	375	190
2/3 cup	150 ml	12 ounces	350 g	400	200
3/4 cup	175 ml	1 pound	450 g	425	220
1 cup	250 ml	2 1/4 pounds	1 kg	450	230

About the Authors

Linda K. Jackson is a senior advertising and marketing executive
in the food and beverage industry. It is her sweet tooth and love for baking, however,
that fuels her creative energy to spend time on the weekends making delightful meringue
treats that ensure many a dinner invitation with the caveat, "You'll bring dessert, right?"
Linda lives in Los Angeles with her husband and two children.

Jennifer Evans Gardner is a food, travel, and lifestyle writer who contributes to
The LA Times, The Huffington Post, Zagat, and other publications. She owns
Little Feet in the Kitchen cooking school for children and is the author of
Barefoot in the Kitchen: The Pregnancy Survival Cookbook and *Bitchin' in the Kitchen:
The PMS Survival Cookbook.* She lives in Los Angeles with her son and Boston terrier.